The Course Companion
for the
BHS Preliminary Teaching
Test

THE COURSE COMPANION FOR THE BHS PRELIMINARY TEACHING TEST

MAXINE CAVE

J. A. ALLEN
London

For Trebor
because he's the best

British Library Cataloguing-in-Publication Data.
A catalogue record for this book is available from the British Library.

ISBN 0–85131–685–9

798 . 2307/CAV ·

Published in Great Britain in 1997 by
J. A. Allen & Company Limited
1 Lower Grosvenor Place
London SW1W 0EL

Typesetting and production Bill Ireson
Illustrations Maggie Raynor
Cover design Nancy Lawrence
Printed in Hong Kong

Contents

Introduction

In this book I have set out to cover the syllabus of the Preliminary Teaching Test (PTT), which is the first teaching examination of the British Horse Society (BHS).

I have also included general information which I think is useful to anyone starting out as an instructor.

To be a good instructor it is vital to gain as much practical teaching experience as possible. This is difficult to do when one is just starting out, as it is necessary to find willing "guinea pig" pupils available for practice sessions.

A great deal of experience can be gained by assisting at Pony Club or riding club rallies and in riding schools. Take this opportunity to watch experienced, qualified, instructors at work. Listen to the comments they make and the instructions they give, while watching the pupils and developing an eye for observing rider problems, and the techniques used to help and correct them. As an assistant, practise putting out poles and jumps at correct distances for a variety of horses, ponies, and riders.

Whenever possible, attend events and demonstrations, as much valuable information and up-to-date ideas can be gained from watching top riders and trainers competing and demonstrating their skills.

If you can also take part yourself in competitions you will learn a great deal almost without realising it. This type of experience will help you to prepare other riders for competitive events.

When watching and helping, always ask yourself, why was that correction made, when should that exercise be used, how should that movement be ridden, which aids should be applied, and so on. In this way you will develop understanding, and it is only through really understanding the subject that you can teach it to someone else.

When riding or receiving lessons yourself, you need to think about how you are riding various exercises, and practise putting into words how you apply the aids, correct your position, prepare for a transition, and so on.

Through gaining as much practice as possible in teaching riders and horses of various levels and abilities, you will begin to become an instructor, and be ready for the first step on the teaching qualification ladder.

1 The Qualities Required in a Good Instructor

Personality

This is one area which may be difficult for some instructors to develop as it is a question of each individual's natural outlook on life. Experience brings confidence and maturity, which in turn bring out a more full and rounded personality. However, those who are naturally outgoing and confident, and perhaps a little bit extrovert, will find it easier to become successful as a teacher.

a. A naturally authoritative manner, without being overbearing or "bossy", will instil confidence in the pupils and encourage them to listen to, and believe in, what they are being told.
b. A sense of humour is essential to help everyone relax and enjoy the learning process, but an instructor should never be sarcastic.
c. An understanding attitude towards pupils' needs and problems, and an ability to empathise with them, will help to maintain good pupil/instructor relations.
d. Patience is vital as all pupils will learn at a different rate, and some will find certain exercises difficult to grasp. This doesn't mean that a pupil lacks intelligence, it usually just means that he or she has so much to concentrate on to begin with, that they cannot always cope with the rapid input of information.

Knowledge

a. If the instructor is to give an informative lesson, and provide correct information to their pupils, then a thorough knowledge of the subjects to be covered is vital. Misinformation or lack of understanding on the part of the instructor will lead to poor progress from the pupils, and eventually a lack of belief in their instructor.

b. As we should all be learning and improving our level of knowledge on a continuous basis, it is the duty of an instructor to be informed in the latest trends and techniques so as to keep up to date. Likewise, the instructor should be practiced in the ability to perform and therefore demonstrate all aspects of teaching, unless perhaps injury prevents him or her from so doing which is sometimes the case.

c. Instructors need to be adept at explaining exercises and corrections clearly and in many different ways. For example, when correcting a common fault such as a rider's tendency to tense their seat muscles and perch in the saddle, the instructor may say: "Relax your seat muscles", or "Let yourself sink into the saddle", or "Try to feel that you are spreading your seat across the saddle." These are all slightly different phrases that can be used to produce the same effect, but one of those phrases may work for one particular rider more than another. The instructor should continually try to add to his or her repertoire of phrases and see which work best for pupils.

Presentation

a. Through smart and practical turnout, an instructor demonstrates to pupils an interest in them and a keenness to become involved in teaching their group to a high standard. Scruffy, or sloppy turnout gives the impression of someone who doesn't really care.

b. Good voice production is essential. If the instructor has a squeaky, monotonous, or very quiet voice, riders will have difficulty in concentrating on and hearing the instructions given. Every effort must be made to develop a clear, audible, voice. Try not to shout from your throat, but see if you can bring your voice from lower down in your lungs. Try to modulate your voice and emphasise various words so you put interest and expression into what you are saying.

2 Lesson Structure

All lessons, whether a half-hour lead rein, or an hour's group, should have a plan based around a simple structure. For the more experienced instructor, planning and structuring a lesson will become second nature. He or she will only have to put more thought into special lessons – like, perhaps, a Pony Club or riding club rally, for which they may be asked to teach a specific subject to pupils they have not met before.

To make the structure easy to remember, the following headings are a series of words ending in TION.

Introduction

a. The introduction should take up one to five minutes at the beginning of the lesson. The time taken will depend on whether you know the pupil and their horse, and whether you have one or more pupils. Care should be taken to find out all relevant information, and make the necessary safety checks, without spending so long on the introduction that the pupils become bored and develop negative feelings towards you.

b. All lessons require an introduction. It is basically the meeting between pupil and instructor. For those that know each other it will be a simple greeting like: "Hello, how are you today?"

c. If the instructor is meeting a pupil for the first time, then he or she will need to introduce themselves and explain who they are. Then, they should find out all they can about the pupil. Questions to be asked may include:

— Have you ridden before?
— How much riding have you done and what type of activities have

you experienced, for example, jumping, hacking, etc.?
— Have you taken any riding examinations or tests?
— How old are you (if a child)?
— What type of horses do you have experience of?
— Do you have any medical problems (for example, asthma or arthritis) that it would be helpful for me to know about?
— What do you hope to gain from your riding lessons, for example: all-round improvement; to be competent to hack out; to be able to jump in affiliated competitions, etc.?
— Is this your horse: how old is he; how experienced is he; how long have you had him, etc.?

d. For group lessons, the instructor should ask the pupils some of the above questions, while checking their horses' tack. As the instructor is responsible for the ride, he or she must check that girths are firm, that all leather work is correctly buckled, and that each horse is safely turned out and that tack fits comfortably. This is especially important if you are teaching pupils who have prepared the horses themselves. The riders should feel involved in this part of the lesson, as it is an essential part of their education; each rider should make sure their tack is safe and comfortable for both themselves and their horse.

Explanation

a. This part of the lesson should take no more than one or two minutes, but it is very important that pupils know what the aims of the lesson are. They will improve more quickly if they understand why they are riding various movements, and will carry out the exercises to a higher standard if they know what they are aiming for.

b. For first-time riders, or pupils visiting your riding centre for the first time, the explanation should include where the lesson will be taking place, and any rules or routines you have. For example, "We lead the horses into the indoor school and mount up in there", or, "We take the horses round to the mounting block, rather than mounting from the ground", and so on.

c. For pupils you know, the explanation will include an outline of your aims for those riders today. For example, you may say, "Today, I am going to begin by warming up both horses and riders, then I am going on to concentrate on grid work and improving your forward position."

d. An explanation should always follow the introduction, but further explanations may be needed at various points throughout the lesson when problems arise and points need clarifying.

Demonstration

a. A demonstration can make clear a subject that is difficult for the pupils to visualise. For example, you may demonstrate a turn on the forehand or the forward position.

b. Demonstrations should take no more than one or two minutes, otherwise pupils become bored and impatient because they want to get on with riding.

c. As with explanations, a demonstration can be used at various intervals throughout the lesson as necessary. You could stop the lesson to demonstrate to a rider where he or she is making mistakes, and how to put them right.

Execution

I use this word to encompass the main part of the lesson, where the riders are now working through the exercises and practising the movements under the guidance of the instructor. For an hour's lesson this may take up half to three-quarters of the hour.

Interrogation

a. Interrogation is questioning time. This section of the lesson must take place well before the end, and may take one to five minutes, depending on the number of riders.

b. The instructor should ask the pupils questions in order to find out if they have fully understood the exercises taught. Questions should also be asked about the way the pupils' horses were working for them. The instructor will then gain a clear picture of exercises that need more practice and/or explanation.

c. At the same time, pupils should be invited to ask questions about any aspect of the lesson that may have confused them.

d. The interrogation section can be used at several stages throughout the lesson if the instructor or pupils feel the need. An experienced instructor will know when to stop and ask questions in order to check and clarify knowledge.

e. It is important not to leave all questions until the end of the lesson, as there will be no time left to practise any aspect of the lesson that was not clearly understood. Also, both the rider's and instructor's time will have been wasted if the riders have been working at an exercise incorrectly due to misunderstanding.

Repetition

a. Repetition may take up quite a large part of the lesson – perhaps 15 to 20 minutes of an hour's lesson. This is the section when riders practise exercises again, after asking questions and having their understanding checked and clarified.

b. This section is likely to be repeated several times throughout the lesson, depending on the subject matter and on the number of pupils involved.

c. It is important to leave time for repetition, as this is often the time when an exercise is ridden showing improvement, and horse and rider can then move on to something else and leave the last exercise on a good note. It is equally important not to repeat something so often that horse and rider become bored and tired and begin to deteriorate.

Conclusion

a. One to five minutes should be left at the end of the lesson for the instructor to summarise for each rider the problems and improvement shown in today's lesson.

b. The instructor should try to leave each rider with a sense of having achieved, and with an aim to work towards for their next lesson.

c. There may also be some last minute questions at this stage, so the instructor should invite pupils to ask about anything that concerns them.

It should be apparent from the above that each lesson needs to be structured in such a way that there is enough time allocated to each aspect of the lesson, and not too much time spent on one area so that another area suffers. The instructor should have a plan of what subject matter he or she wants to cover, and how far to progress in the given time. This plan should then be carried out within the framework of the structure described. The instructor always needs to be prepared to be flexible with such a plan, as horses and riders may not perform in the way anticipated. The structure can be applied to stable management lectures as well as to all types of riding lessons.

3   Terms and Commands

When teaching, recognised terms and commands are used which enable the instructor to communicate with pupils and keep control of a ride. Although there may be slight variations in this, if all instructors learn a standard set of terms and commands, they can be sure of being understood wherever they teach. This saves on lengthy explanations and is an aid to good ride control.

School rules

Most lessons will take place in an indoor or an outdoor school – these are sometimes referred to respectively as an arena or an outdoor manege. When a purpose-built school is not available, an area should be marked out in a field with the school letters correctly placed.

a. Before entering an occupied school, knock at the door, or make your presence known at the gate and check that it is safe to enter. The instructor conducting the lesson must be given time to bring the ride forward to a safe pace and clear the entrance to allow you to enter safely.
b. Doors/gates at the entrance should always be securely closed when the school is occupied. An accident could easily occur if a horse decided to try and "duck out" through an open doorway.
c. In the school, always leave the outer track clear for those working in faster gaits, so move onto an inner track before walking or halting. If mounting, dismounting, adjusting stirrups, etc., then stand in the middle of the school well out of the way of other riders.
d. If passing another rider who is going in the opposite direction to you, pass left hand to left hand.

If mounting, dismounting, etc., stand in the middle of the school, well out of the way of other riders.

Pass left hand to left hand.

e. Give way to riders riding lateral work.
f. Circle away from other riders before getting too close and look up and remain alert at all times.
g. If a horse is being lunged in the school (without a rider), pass it riding in the opposite direction to which it is being lunged as you are less likely to be kicked. If it is a mature, sensible horse being used for lungeing a rider, then you can pass it in the same direction as it is working on the lunge.
h. Before leaving the school, pick out your horse's feet, and check that other riders are aware that you are leaving and that it is safe to do so.

Terms

a. Letters B and E may be referred to as the half markers.
b. Letters K, H, M, and F may be referred to as the quarter markers.
c. A straight line running from A to C is the centre line.
d. Running parallel to the centre line are the quarter and three-quarter lines, representing a point midway between the centre line and the side of the school.
e. In some schools, additional coloured or shaped markers are placed on the walls to represent the quarter and three-quarter lines and also the tangent points of a 20m circle.
f. The very centre of the school is called X.
g. The outer track is a track around the outer edge of the school which follows the boards or rails. The inner track is the term used for riding a track just within the outer track.
h. In a group lesson the riders are referred to as "the ride".
i. Riding as a ride can be in "closed order", which means each rider follows behind the other a set distance away. The usual distance set is the length of one horse. Or, the ride can work in "open order", which means the riders space themselves out as far apart from each other as possible, and ride individually by circling away from each other before they get too close to the horse in front.
j. "Go large" is the term used to send the riders out around the outer track to continue around the whole school.

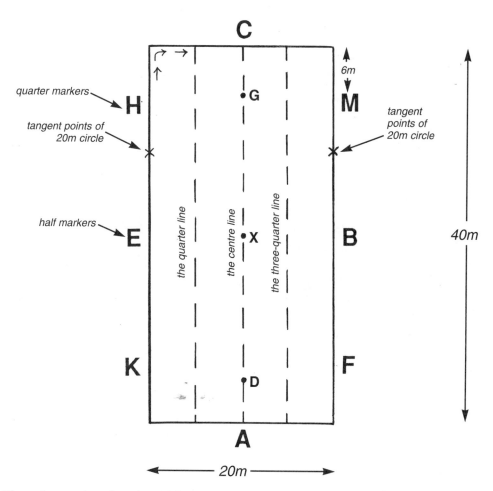

Dimensions and markers for a riding arena, 20mx40m. **D** *and* **G** *are points on the centre line level with the quarter markers.*

k. "In succession" means each rider is to carry out the exercise set, one after the other. So as one person completes an exercise, the next in line begins the exercise.

l. "Lead file" refers to the rider at the front of the ride leading the group; and "rear file" refers to the rider bringing up the rear.

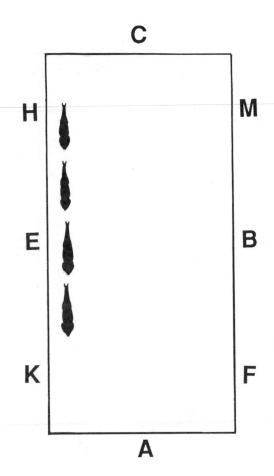

Closed order.

m. "Inside" and "Outside" refer to the inside and outside of the movement. So, when riding round the school, the rider's inside leg and hand
are the leg and hand that are towards the middle of the school, and the
outside leg and hand are those nearest the boards of the school.

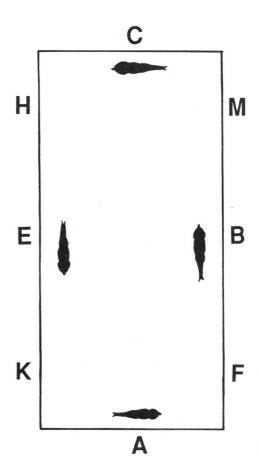

Open order.

n. "Left/right rein" refers to the direction. If riding round the school in a clockwise direction, the riders are on the right rein. (The right rein is on the inside.) An anti-clockwise direction means riding on the left rein.

o. "Changing the rein", therefore refers to changing direction.

p. The horse's left-hand side is referred to as the "nearside", and the horse's right-hand side is referred to as the "offside".

Commands

Although the word "command" sounds rather fierce and not very polite, it is essential that the instructor has complete control of the ride in order for everyone to learn and ride safely. The instructor may often be aware of a potentially dangerous situation that all the riders are not aware of. In this instance, if the riders respond to the instructor's command then the danger can be avoided. This is why commands are used rather than a "Please would you?"

Before each command, the instructor must give a preparatory command so the riders can prepare themselves and their horses for the exercise to follow. The following are some examples of recognised commands to use.

a. To move off a group lesson that are at halt having just mounted up on the centre line of the school.
Preparation: whole ride, as a ride, keeping one horse's distance between you, prepare to walk forward to the opposite track and track right.
Command: "Whole ride walk march."
b. With the ride at walk in closed order.
Preparation: whole ride prepare to trot.
Command: "Whole ride trot."
c. In order to remind the riders to keep the length of one horse between themselves and the horse in front, the instructor will say, "Keep your distances," and may have to pick out one particular individual who is getting too close, or too far behind. Also, explain to riders how to go about adjusting their distances. The usual format is for the rider to steady his or her pace if getting too close, or cut across the next corner if getting too far behind.
d. For individual riders to take canter to the rear of the ride.
Preparation: lead files in succession prepare to go forward to canter in the next available corner and canter to the rear of the ride.
Command: "Lead file commence."

e. For the ride to return to walk.
    Preparation: whole ride prepare to ride forward to walk.
    Command: "Whole ride walk."

f. To change the rein using the centre line.
    Preparation: whole ride prepare to make a change of rein up the centre line.
    Command: "Lead file, at A turn down the centre line, the rest of the ride follow, and at C track left."

g. To finish the lesson, by bringing all the riders into the centre of the school to line up safely beside each other all facing the same way, you would say, "Lead file, between the E and H markers, make a right turn and halt on the centre line facing the B side of the school. Rest of the ride form a ride on your lead file's right."

h. If the instructor is making a correction to one particular rider, it is helpful to use the rider's name first, in order to gain their attention. For example, it is better to say, "Carol, carry your hands a little higher", rather than, "Carry your hands a little higher, Carol".

i. When making corrections and giving instructions take care with your use of words. With a little thought you can make subtle differences that should have a positive effect on your riders. For example, try to use the word "Forward" before giving the command for a downwards transition, rather than "Back". In this way you encourage riders to ride the horse from leg into hand, rather than pulling back. If you would like a rider to return to walk after a period of trot, say "Forward to walk now", rather than "Back to walk now".

j. Another example is when the instructor talks about riding the horse between leg and hand. Always say "Leg" first, to encourage riders to use their legs fractionally in advance of their rein aids at all times. You should say, "Ride your horse forward from leg into hand", rather than "Keep the horse between hand and leg".

Points to note

1. Commands must be given well in advance. Remember that when you give the command riders will need a few moments to take in what you have said, then will need to prepare both themselves and their horse. If

they are on the move in walk, trot, or canter, they need even more time. So think well ahead and give the command well in advance of when you require the exercise to be carried out.

2. If you need to explain a more complicated exercise, always bring the riders forward to walk or halt. They will find it difficult to concentrate on your explanation if they are, for example, trotting around the school at the time. Also, the horse is bound to "switch off" if it is trotting around the school and its rider's attention is focused elsewhere.

Helpful hints on exam technique

1. Keep commands as short and simple as possible. The riders will find it easier to listen to you and understand what you are saying if you do not complicate the directions you give with an excess of words.

2. Always try to keep your voice bright and interesting. Try not to fall into the trap of "singing" out the commands in a monotonous way. It is very important that your lessons are clear and that your pupils find you enjoyable to listen to.

4 Subjects for Beginner Lessons

Approach to the horse

a. Introduce the riders to their horses. Show them how to approach safely by going to the horse's shoulder.
b. They should never approach the horse from directly in front or behind where it cannot see them clearly and they could startle it.
c. They should always go around the front of the horse if moving from one side to the other, in order to avoid the horse's hind legs which it could kick out with.

Mounting

a. Show pupils how to prepare for mounting, and involve them in each procedure. They should put the reins over their horse's head, then check the girth.

Check and tighten the girth.

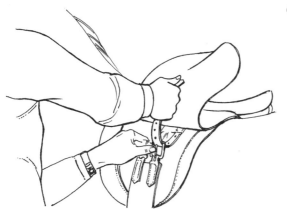

b. Adjust the girth so it is firm and tightened to approximately the same number of holes on each side. Pull each of the horse's forelegs forward, in turn, to ease wrinkles of skin from under the girth, and thereby preventing pinching.

c. Run the stirrups down and check for length by measuring them against the length of the rider's arm. Show them how this is done by putting your knuckles against the stirrup bar, and drawing the stirrup iron up to your armpit. Explain that if the stirrup leathers are the same length as your arm, they will be near to the correct length for you to ride with, although they may need further adjustment once you have mounted. Stand in front of the horse and look to see if the stirrups are level.

d. When mounting it is always a good idea to use a mounting block, thereby preventing strain on the horse's back caused by a rider pulling themselves up from the ground. The mounting block will also prevent the saddle from becoming twisted if riders pull themselves up; when mounting expertly riders should not pull on the horse at all – they should "spring" lightly into the saddle. However, this is not often the case, especially at beginner level.

Pull each foreleg forward in turn to ease wrinkling.

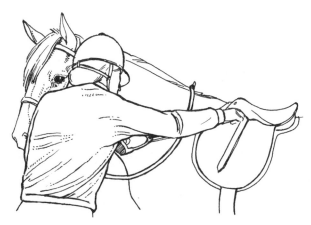

Check the length of the stirrup leathers.

e. Position the horse so that its nearside is alongside the mounting block. The rider should stand on the block and take up the reins in their left hand. By keeping the offside rein a little shorter, the horse is encouraged to keep its back and hindquarters close to the block; this also prevents the horse taking a nip at the rider as he or she mounts.

Mounting from a block.

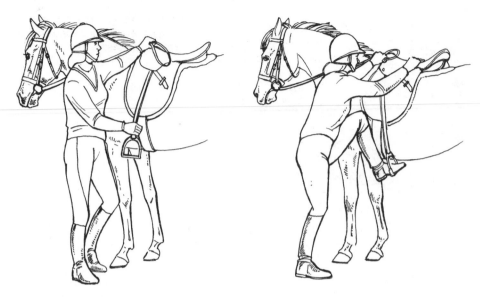

Mounting from the ground.

f. If the rider is carrying a stick, it should be held in the left hand resting down the horse's nearside shoulder. Here the stick will encourage the horse to keep still and not walk forward, as well as be out of the way. The rider can also take hold of a piece of the horse's mane in their left hand, or just rest their hand on the horse's neck, just in front of the withers.

g. The rider should then take the nearside stirrup with their right hand, turning the back edge of the stirrup outwards and turn their body so they face towards the horse's hindquarters. In this way the rider will be more able to keep with the horse should it begin to walk forward, rather than getting left behind with one foot in the stirrup and possibly falling over backwards.

h. Now the rider should place their left foot well into the stirrup and turn their toes slightly down to prevent their foot from digging into the horse's side.

i. With their right hand, the rider reaches across the saddle and takes a light hold on the offside of the saddle at the waist, or pommel. With

Having a leg up. Note that the rider's right hand is placed across the waist of the saddle.

Having a leg up.

one or two hops, they move round towards the horse and spring lightly into the saddle by swinging their right leg over the horse's hind quarters, being careful not to brush a foot against the horse on the way, and lower their seat into the saddle gently.

j.   Having sat down in the saddle, the rider's right foot should be slipped into the stirrup and he or she takes up the reins in both hands.

k.   An assistant can be of help when the rider is mounting. The assistant stands on the offside of the horse and holds its offside rein to encourage it to stay still, while holding the rider's offside stirrup. This will help to keep the saddle central on the horse's back when the rider puts his or her weight into the nearside stirrup.

l.   A leg up can also be a useful way of mounting. The rider should prepare for mounting and take up the reins in the same way as described above, but this time place the stick on the offside of the horse so as to prevent it from poking in the face of the person giving the leg up.

m. The rider's left and right hands should be placed in the same positions, definitely not on the back of the saddle, while the rider faces the saddle, and holds up their left leg by bending it at the knee.

n.   The assistant should place one hand under the rider's left knee, and the other hand just behind it, being careful to bend their own knees rather than bending their back which could cause strain.

o.   The rider then bends a little in the right knee in order to prepare for an upward spring. As the rider springs upward, the assistant adds to the lift by pushing up under the rider's left knee.

p.   As the rider reaches sufficient height they swing their right leg over the back of the horse, in the same way as for mounting described above, then place both feet in the stirrups having landed lightly in the saddle.

q.   The rider should take care not to throw themselves forward over the saddle during the leg up, but concentrate on springing straight up as, having reached a sufficient height, they will then find it easy to swing their leg over the horse.

Dismounting

a.   To dismount, the rider should take both feet out of the stirrups; then

Dismounting. Remember to bend your knees as you land.

take their reins and stick into their left hand and place their right hand on the pommel of the saddle.

b. The rider then leans forward a little and swings the right leg up and over the horse's quarters behind them, springing slightly away from the horse and the saddle before landing lightly with knees bent, to absorb concussion.

Holding and adjusting the reins

a. When holding the reins, the rider should take one rein in each hand, checking that the rein is straight and not twisted, from the bit to their hands.

b. The rein should come in to the hand between the rider's little finger and third finger, up through the hand and out over the index finger. The thumb should be placed gently on top of the rein to keep it from slipping through the rider's hand.

Holding the reins. The thumb is placed gently on top of the rein to keep it from slipping through the rider's hand.

c. The spare loop of rein should hang down the horse's shoulder inside, not over, the rein being held. If it does hang over the rein, it causes interference to the contact with the horse's mouth.

d. To lengthen the reins, the rider should slightly open their fingers and allow the reins to slip through until the required length is achieved.

e. To shorten the reins, the rider uses the thumb and index finger of the right hand, for example, and takes hold of the left rein (where it comes out of the left hand between left thumb and index finger). The rider can then slide the left hand down the rein until they reach the required length. Then repeat the process with the right rein.

Adjusting stirrups

a. When adjusting stirrups the rider should keep their feet in the stirrup irons in order to make sure they are always secure. Then, if the horse begins to walk off, the rider can concentrate on regaining control and not have to worry about trying to find their stirrups at the same time.

b. The rider should lighten their weight in the stirrup iron and pull the buckle of the leathers away from the stirrup bar with one hand, whilst keeping hold of the reins with the other hand.

c. They can then adjust the length of the stirrup leathers, by moving the buckle up or down a few holes, to make them longer or shorter.

d. Now the buckle is pulled back up to the stirrup bar.

e. The stirrup leathers must be straight and not twisted. To help the rider check this, when mounted, the stirrup leather should lie completely flat

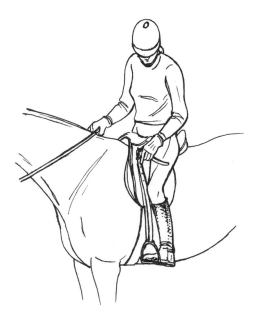

Adjusting stirrups. Riders should keep their feet in the stirrups for security.

and straight, then the front edge of the stirrup iron is turned outwards as the rider puts their foot in the iron.

Checking and tightening the girth

a. To check and tighten the girth when mounted, the rider should keep their feet in the stirrups for the same reason as above, and lift, for example, their left leg forward over the knee roll of the saddle.

b. With their left hand they can lift up the saddle flap which can then be held with their right hand along with the reins, while with their left hand they can pull the girth buckles up one or more holes.

c. If they are unable to tighten the girth by one hole, this usually means it is tight enough already.

Points to note

1. It is important from the outset that you check to see that all procedures you have taught pupils are carried out correctly each time you take them for instruction. If you help and correct pupils in this way, safe and

*Adjusting the girth
when mounted.*

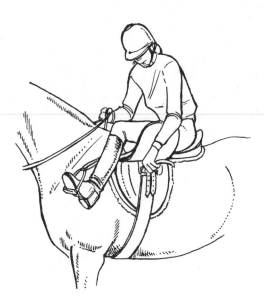

effective ways of carrying out these procedures will become second nature to them.

2. For very young children, keep your explanations very simple, and avoid using words that may not yet be part of their vocabulary. They will be learning all the new equestrian terms anyway, and this will be enough for them to cope with. Find out how old they are. Children develop at different rates, and you may be teaching a four-year-old who is as big as a seven-year-old; in this case you could be expecting too much from the child.

3. Make sure you don't talk down to children – and don't fall into the trap of talking down to adults just because you are teaching them about a subject they are as yet unfamiliar with.

4. Each of the above points will usually need to be demonstrated to pupils to make it clearer for them. You could demonstrate these points yourself, or an assistant can be asked to do so while you talk through the method.

5. Very young children will need to be shown how to hold the reins, by having you place their fingers where they should be, rather than being

expected to interpret your instructions referring to their index fingers, etc.

Common rider faults and problems

1. Riders often forget to keep hold of the horse while they are moving around it. Show them how to keep one arm linked through the reins, and keep reminding them not to let the horse go.

2. A common fault when mounting is that of the rider holding onto the back of the saddle. This should not be allowed, as the saddle will be pulled into a twisted position on the horse's back and the rider cannot swing their leg over the back of the saddle if their hand and arm are in the way. They will have to let go at some point, which causes an unbalancing effect which, in turn, is uncomfortable for the horse. Also, riders often land very heavily in the saddle when trying to master the art of mounting. The instructor should stress the need to land lightly, and help the rider to do so.

3. Riders may not be able to spring away from the horse to begin with, when dismounting, and could be inclined to slither down the side of the horse, hanging on to the saddle. Try to discourage this, pointing out that it is uncomfortable for the horse. At the other extreme, riders may spring too far, lose balance, and begin falling backwards. Make sure you are there with a steadying hand.

4. Riders often shift their weight right back in the saddle when adjusting stirrups, which is not good practice and should be discouraged.

The next stage in a beginner lesson

The correct riding position

a. Riders should be taught to sit in the deepest part of the saddle, with their weight central. They should sit up straight, remain relaxed, and try to imagine a straight line, perpendicular to the ground, running

A good balanced position.

from their ear, to their shoulder, down to their hip, and then on down to their heel.

b. A second straight line is drawn from the elbow to the rider's little finger, and on down the rein to the bit. If the rider learns to align their body in this way, they will have a good basic position in the saddle.

c. A demonstration of the correct position, pointing out the two straight lines, will be helpful to the rider.

The natural aids and how to begin using them

a. Explain to the rider that the natural aids are the rider's voice, legs and hands, while artificial aids are whip and spurs. Thought can also be included as a natural aid if you wish.

b. Explain that the rider's legs are used to ask the horse to move forward and sideways, while their hands on the reins guide the horse and help to control the amount of forward movement. Their voice is an extra aid to help the horse understand what the rider is asking them to do.

c. Teach the rider to take up a contact with the reins and use their legs in a nudging action, to ask the horse to walk on. They can also use their voice, and say "Walk on" to the horse.

d. Once the rider has experienced the feel of the walk, explain the gait to them, going into more depth for adult riders and just outline the basics for small children.

e. The walk is a four-time gait. The horse picks up each of its feet in turn: for example, near fore followed by off hind, then off fore followed by near hind. If you listen to the footfalls you should be able to hear four distinct beats.

f. In walk, the horse's head will nod up and down in a regular rhythm and its back will be moving in a regular motion with each step. Therefore, the rider will need to allow their hands and arms to move, also their back and seat, in order not to restrict the horse.

g. To return to the halt, the rider should keep their legs still against the horse's side, no longer nudging, and also keep their hands still, no longer following the movement. As they try to sit still and keep their legs and hands still, they can also use their voice to say "Whoa, and halt." Once the horse has halted they should relax and reward the horse with a pat.

h. When teaching the rider to steer the horse, encourage them to look round to where they want to go, to use their inside leg quite firmly, in order to give the horse something to bend around so it does not just cut the corner, and gently open the inside rein to guide the horse in the required direction.

Points to note

1. The instructor will need to make constant corrections to the riders' mounted position, while helping them to achieve the required skills.
2. Points "a." to "h." above explain how to start, stop and steer (the first basics a beginner needs to learn), in a very simple way. Much of riding is hard to explain as it is all about feel and balance. Greater under-

standing will gradually develop, and the idea of riding from the inside leg to the outside rein will take many hours of practice, and therefore will make little sense to the beginner rider at this stage.

3. I feel it is best to tell riders to nudge with their legs to give the aid. If told to "squeeze", they often become rigid in the saddle and literally squeeze themselves upwards and out of the seat. The type of horse or pony they will be riding at this level is unlikely to respond to a light aid, but if told to "kick", they can become too rough.

4. Likewise, if told to follow the horse's movement with their hands and arms, and then to cease following, or to open the inside rein to guide, they are more likely to be gentle with the horse than if they are told to "pull" on the reins.

5. Throughout the lesson the instructor must explain each new equestrian term used. For example, "nearside" and "offside", "transitions", and "changes of rein".

Common rider faults and problems

1. At this stage riders will find it difficult to coordinate their leg and rein aids. Their hands will often pull back on the reins while they are trying to urge their horse forward with their legs, thus making it more difficult to succeed in getting the horse to walk on.

2. Riders at this stage have great difficulty also in using their legs in an inwards direction. They usually end up swinging their legs back along their horse's sides, which has no effect at all on their quiet mount.

3. The efforts made to apply the aids often result in tension and gripping with the knees which can cause the rider to tip forward into a slumped position, or lean backwards into an armchair seat. This results in a loss of balance and further lack of effectiveness.

Subjects to move on to as the beginner progresses

The trot

a. Depending on the age of the rider, explain that the trot is a faster gait than the walk, and is a two-time gait in which the horse moves one diagonal pair of legs, then the other pair. Point out which legs move together to show what is meant by a "diagonal pair".

b. Explain that there is a moment of suspension, when the horse has none of its hooves on the ground, as it changes from one pair of legs to the other. This makes the trot a slightly bumpy gait for a beginner rider, but with practice they will learn to ride it smoothly.

c. Prepare the rider for trot by having him or her hold on to the pommel of the saddle. Encourage them to use their legs more actively and firmly to indicate to the horse that they are asking for trot, and tell them to use their voice by saying, "Trrrot."

d. They should be told to sit still in the saddle and to try and maintain the correct riding position.

e. The instructor should encourage the horse to trot and keep to a straight line, as trotting around corners will be very unbalancing for the rider the first time. Also, the instructor must take care to be ready to hold on to the rider if they begin to lose balance, and to bring the horse forward to walk after a short distance.

f. Having given the rider a chance to feel the trot movement, two or three times, go on to explain that rising to the trot is used to make the trot less tiring and more comfortable for both horse and rider. If possible, show your pupil another rider demonstrating the trot "rising".

g. Go on to teach the rider how to stand up and sit down in a controlled manner while the horse is at halt. It will help if they can hold a piece of mane or a neck strap. Explain that they must keep their lower leg in a correct position in order to maintain their balance, and it will help them if they lean forwards a little, to begin with.

h. Once they can stand and sit without loss of balance, go on to practise this in walk, then eventually in the trot. It will help some riders if the instructor calls out "Up, down" for children, and perhaps "One, two" for adults, to help them slot into rhythm with the horse.

i. Don't try to teach the rider about rising with the correct diagonal until they have mastered rising to the trot and can carry out the movement quite smoothly.

j. Riders should be taught to try and use their leg aids as they sit down

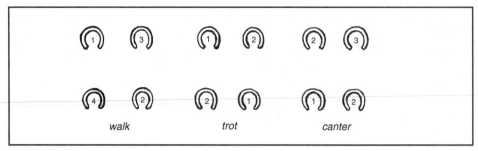

The sequence of footfalls in walk, trot and canter. This sequence is for the right canter lead.

in the saddle with each beat of the trot, as this is when their legs are closest and most effective.

Points to note
1. Riders need to be shown how to hold the front of the saddle correctly. They should tuck their fingers under the front arch of the pommel, and lift the palm of their hand away from the saddle. As they pull up under the pommel, they will pull themselves down into the saddle. If they rest the palm of their hand on the pommel, they will end up pushing down on the pommel, which will actually push them up and out of the saddle, defeating the object of the exercise.
2. The adult rider, especially, will need constant reminders to relax each part of their body. Often without realising it, they will be gripping tightly with their knees, thighs and calves, or tensing their shoulder, back and seat muscles. All of this tension will make it more difficult for the rider to achieve improvement. Keep correcting their position and explain that this is the most balanced and effective way to sit.

Common rider faults and problems
1. As riders first try to stand up in their stirrups, they push against their stirrup irons and their lower leg shoots forward, resulting in an immediate thump back down in the saddle. You can help individuals by holding on to one of their ankles, to keep their lower leg in place.

2. If a rider is finding it hard to balance he or she may clutch at the reins and try to pull themselves up. As they do this, their hands come higher and higher at the same time, hence the necessity to have them holding on to a neck strap or the saddle.

3. Once they begin to get the idea, riders may stand and sit too slowly, missing a trot beat each time, or sitting for too long each time so they bump in the saddle and lose balance.

4. Riders usually have great difficulty in coordinating their leg aids while trying to keep to a regular trot rhythm, and will find steering even more difficult. However, you should still have them on a lead rein at this stage, so you can help to keep the horse trotting and steer for them.

5. To rise to the trot, riders often try to lift themselves out of the saddle, by hunching their shoulders. This action causes tension and will tip them forward.

Trotting diagonals

a. Once the rider has mastered the art of rising to the trot fluently, you can teach them about rising with the correct diagonal.

b. First explain that you are referring to the trot gait in which the horse moves its legs in diagonal pairs, as explained previously. Each time the rider rises and sits he or she is moving up and down as one particular diagonal pair of legs is being moved forward by the horse.

c. If the rider always moves up and down with one pair of legs, the horse will develop stronger muscles with the pair of legs which support the rider. This will lead to uneven development and one-sidedness in the horse.

d. The rider, therefore, needs to learn to identify which diagonal pair they are rising and sitting with, and be able to change from one pair to the other.

e. When the horse is moving on a straight line, for example when out hacking, the rider can change from one diagonal to the other, as they wish, trying to make sure they use each diagonal evenly throughout the hack.

f. When riding in a school in a particular direction, it helps the horse to maintain its balance if the rider rises with the left diagonal when on the right rein, and right diagonal when on the left rein.

g. Right and left diagonal, refers to the forelimb which the rider is moving with. For example, when on the right rein the rider should rise up and down with the left diagonal, which is the near fore and off hind together. This means that when the rider sits, the horse's inside hind leg is on the ground. The rider is able to use his or her leg aids more effectively at the very moment of sitting down. This, therefore, encourages the inside hind to be lifted forward more actively.

h. When the horse's inside hind leg is on the ground it is momentarily supporting the rider's weight and, by the action of the rider rising, is given the freedom to move forward more easily. This helps the horse to maintain its balance.

i. To help the rider to identify which diagonal they are rising with, begin in walk and tell the rider to look down (without leaning over) at the horse's outside shoulder, to see if they can see the shoulder appearing to move forward and back. Walk beside the horse and point out to the rider what you mean, if necessary.

j. Explain that the same motion will be seen at trot, but it will happen more quickly. The rider is to try to rise up when the shoulder goes forward, and down when the shoulder seems to be going back.

k. If the rider is not in time with the outside shoulder, then they need to try and sit for one extra beat in the saddle, then continue rising. This will change them on to the correct diagonal.

Points to note

1. A demonstration of how to change diagonal will be helpful to the rider. At the same time, coloured bandages or boots could be used to help the rider see another rider rising with the correct diagonal. For example, put white boots on the near fore and off hind, and black boots on the off fore and near hind. Then let the rider sit and watch an experienced rider trot around the school changing the rein and changing diagonal.

2. You should explain to the rider that, as soon as they can, they should cease looking down to check their diagonal as it will tend to unbalance

them. They need to develop a feel for when the diagonal is correct or not.

3. Tell the rider that changing the diagonal can slightly unbalance the horse, so they need to change diagonal at an appropriate point. For example, when riding diagonally across the school to change the rein, they should change the diagonal just as they are reaching the opposite track. If they change the diagonal at X, then the horse may be made to wobble slightly off line.

Common rider faults and problems
1. When changing diagonal to begin with, the rider will often sit for too long in the saddle and not change diagonal at all.
2. Very young children may not quite grasp what they are looking for, and find it difficult to recognise the diagonal on a quick striding little pony.
3. The rider is so intent on looking for the diagonal that he or she forgets to use their legs, and loses coordination, so the horse keeps falling into walk again.
4. Riders frequently lose balance when trying to change diagonal, and need guidance in how to check their positions and prepare themselves.

Canter

a. Explain to the rider that the canter is a three-time gait. For example, the horse may begin the canter stride with its near hind. This is followed by the off hind and near fore together, then lastly the off fore. There is a moment of suspension before the sequence is repeated.

b. In canter the horse has a leading leg. The sequence outlined above is for right canter, the final leg in the sequence being the leading leg. It stretches a little further forward and leads the horse smoothly around corners in that direction.

c. For riders to ask for right canter, they should establish an active trot on the right rein. When they approach a corner, take sitting trot and apply their inside leg firmly in a forward driving aid at the girth. Their outside leg should slide a little behind the girth and nudge to encourage the outside hind leg to begin the canter sequence. At the same time the rider must maintain a steady contact with the reins, but follow the horse's movement into canter, and keep their upper body in a good balanced position.

d. The rider should keep his or her seat in the saddle and follow the canter movement with supple back and hips. Their leg aids should continue to encourage the horse to maintain the canter, and they must follow the movement of the horse's head and neck with an elastic rein contact.

e. A demonstration of the canter, for the riders to watch, will be very helpful. Include showing them how to sit to the trot to enable a rider to apply clear canter aids, and how a rider should steady the canter before returning to trot, then sit to the trot while re-balancing the horse after the canter.

f. As with diagonals, it is important that the horse uses both canter leads evenly, to prevent it from developing unevenly.

g. Most horses will favour one particular canter lead, rather as humans are right-handed and left-handed. They will tend to try and lead with this leg unless asked to do otherwise. When out hacking, the rider should try to ask the horse to use both canter leads by alternating from one to the other for each canter.

h. The rider needs to develop a feel for which leg the horse is leading with. But, just as with trotting diagonals, don't worry the rider with this too much, until they have mastered the basic transition into canter and are able to sit with the gait fairly smoothly.

i. Having explained to the beginner rider the canter gait, and demonstrated the correct procedure for asking for canter on a named leg, how to ride the canter and return to trot, you will need to go on to explain that you are going to simplify the procedure for the first few canters they ride, otherwise they will find it too much to cope with at once.

j. For the beginner rider to ask the horse to canter for the first time, tell them to encourage the horse into a really forward going trot. Just as they come to the designated corner, tell them to try to sit down in the saddle, hold the neck strap, and use their legs firmly. At the same time you will say "Canter" to help the horse understand.

k. If successful in achieving the canter, the beginner should try to sit in the saddle as shown in the demonstration, and keep using their legs.

l. At the end of the long side of the school it is best if the horse returns to trot, as the rider may find cantering around the corner rather unbalancing to begin with. Explain this to the rider, and tell them to just sit quietly, keep their legs still, and allow the horse to make the transition into trot. You can help to steady the horse with your voice.

m. Warn the rider that the return to trot may be a little bumpy. To help them keep balance and not bump on the horse's back, they should be encouraged to resume rising to the trot straight away.

Points to note

1. Beginner riders will need constant help and correction through the transitions to and from canter, and during the canter itself. Remember that this work will be very tiring for them. Take frequent breaks to check their understanding and ask them what they are finding most difficult.

2. Children on small ponies may be led in canter if the instructor or helper is able to run with the pony. This can be very helpful as some ponies have a tendency to set off rather fast, and if the child panics the pony will probably get faster.

Common rider faults and problems

1. When making the extra effort to ask the horse to canter, the rider will tend to tip forward, losing balance and rein contact. This throws the horse on its forehand and leads to it running in trot rather than striking off into canter.

2. As the horse steps into canter, the rider tips forward which brings their seat out of the saddle. They are unable to follow the canter movement, and bump up and down in the saddle. This is very uncomfortable for the horse and makes the rider very unbalanced and insecure.

3. The rider tries to keep his or her seat in the saddle by leaning back. This puts them behind the movement, and their legs slip forward into an

ineffective position. Again, they become unbalanced and insecure.

4. The rider grips tightly with his or her legs for security, which results in their heels drawing up and possible loss of one or both stirrups. This leaves them out of balance and insecure.

5. The rider forgets to hold the neck strap or saddle and clutches at the reins with their hands getting higher, causing the usual loss of balance and security.

6. More experienced riders may sit quite well in canter, but allow their seats to slip to the outside. This causes them to lean in and collapse their inside hip, which is unbalancing for the horse. The rider is less effective in this position and will block free forward movement of the inside hind leg.

5 Physical Exercises

The purpose

a. Rider exercises can be a useful way of warming-up, and loosening-up, the rider's muscles. Just as we expect the horse to need warming-up before being asked to work on more advanced exercises, so riders should be aware of warming-up their own body, so they can work with their horse in a relaxed and supple manner.
b. For children, particularly, exercises when mounted represent a fun part of the lesson. At the same time, almost without realising it, they are gaining confidence on the horse, and improving their coordination.
c. Exercises can be used to improve the rider's position, and help the rider to feel when they are sitting correctly.
d. Whilst the instructor concentrates on rider exercises the horses have a chance to relax and have a well-earned breather. Therefore, exercises can help in the pacing of a lesson.

Dangers to be aware of

a. Each individual rider's physical ability must be considered. Some riders will be more supple than others, and more able to carry out a particular exercise. When explaining the exercise to be carried out, the instructor should stress that each individual should try to stretch a little, but cease the exercise before causing themselves discomfort. Many riders get cramp from over-doing some exercises. This can be very painful and cause muscle damage. It can also be dangerous if the horse is unnerved by the rider's discomfort.

b. Each rider's conformation should be noted by the instructor, and taken into consideration with regard to each exercise. For example, a female rider who has narrow hips and legs set so her knees turn close together, will have difficulty in stretching her legs around the horse, and great difficulty in carrying out the "legs away" exercise.

c. In order to be safe, most exercises should only be conducted at halt or walk. Riders can easily be jolted, and physically damaged, if they lose balance having been asked to carry out an exercise at trot, for example. For this same reason, it is better not to use exercises which involve moving the head around in circles or from side to side.

d. The instructor must be sure that the horses are familiar with riders doing various exercises when mounted. A young horse could easily take fright if its rider began circling an arm – something it had never experienced before.

e. Some of the fun exercises, such as "round the world", that have been enjoyed by children for many years, should only be carried out at halt and with an assistant holding the pony. The instructor must also be sure that the pony is familiar with the exercises. In these safety conscious times, when people are sued at the drop of a hat, the instructor should not take any chances. What the children do in their own time, and on their own ponies, is up to them and their parents.

The Exercises

Shoulder shrugging

The rider's shoulders are drawn up to the ears and then rotated back and down. The exercise should be done slowly, just two or three times, with emphasis on pulling the shoulders well back and down, whilst maintaining a correct balanced seat. The rider should feel a loosening and release of any tension around the shoulders and neck.

WHEN TO USE THE EXERCISE

a. If the rider has poor posture with rounded shoulders, this exercise should help.

b. This is a useful exercise if the rider appears to be tense and nervous, as it can help them to release some of their tension.

c. Also, it is a good exercise to use during a lunge, or lead rein lesson, when the rider doesn't need to keep a steady contact on the reins, and will help with the problems noted in "a." and "b." above.

d. When the horses are being ridden on a long rein at the beginning of a group lesson, or during a rest phase, this exercise could be used to help with the rider warm-up, or to relax riders when the horses are having a break.

Arm circling

The inside arm is stretched up, round and back, in a large circle. The exercise should be done slowly, with emphasis on the rider keeping a correct balanced position, whilst stretching up, and keeping their arm straight as they circle back and down. The rider should feel a stretching of the upper

Arm circling.

body muscles and a loosening of the shoulder. It should be repeated two or three times, on each rein.

WHEN TO USE THE EXERCISE
a. A good exercise to use during any lesson, as the reins can be taken in one hand leaving the other arm free to be circled. Riders who tend to tip forward, or slump in the saddle, will benefit from this exercise.
b. The inside arm is circled, as this brings the inside shoulder back a little, so helping the rider to turn in the direction of the movement. By changing the rein and repeating the exercise, each side of the body is stretched.
c. This exercise can also be useful to correct a rider who sits crookedly, with one shoulder much further forward than the other. In this case, the exercise could just be used on one rein, or repeated a few more times with the side of the body that the rider holds crookedly.

Toe touching

The rider takes the reins in one hand and with his or her free hand reaches down to the corresponding toe: for example, right hand to right toe. The rider can also be asked to reach across to the opposite toe: for example, right hand to left toe. A variation on this theme would be to reach forward and touch the pony's ears, or reach behind to touch the pony's tail. The rider must keep a correct leg position, and not allow his or her lower leg to swing forward or backwards. This exercise should not be done hurriedly.

WHEN TO USE THE EXERCISE
a. This exercise has the disadvantage of bringing the rider's seat out of the saddle. Because of this it is best used as a fun, confidence-giving exercise for children as a group exercise, or used during a lead rein lesson.
b. For children with poor coordination, it is a good exercise as long as the instructor ensures the riders keep their lower leg position.
c. For a nervous child, during a lead rein lesson, it can be used to give

him or her the confidence to move on the pony and gradually feel more secure.

Legs away

This exercise is carried out when the stirrups have been quit and crossed over the front of the saddle.

With one hand resting on the pommel of the saddle, the rider lifts one leg at a time, up and away from the saddle. The rider's upper body and seat should remain in a correct balanced position. The legs should be lifted out from the hip joint, with the knees a little bent and lifted, then gently lowered back into a correct position on the horse's side.

Legs away. The rider lifts one or both legs away from the saddle to help open the hip joint and improve the depth of seat.

The rider's legs should only be lifted away as far as is comfortable for the rider.

WHEN TO USE THE EXERCISE
a. In group, private or lunge lessons the rider can carry out this exercise at halt or walk. It helps to loosen the hip joint and put the legs in a good position.
b. Riders who tend to grip with their knees and thighs and draw their legs too far forward, will benefit from this exercise.
c. The instructor must take care not to demand too much from this exercise with novice and older riders who are likely to be less supple than younger and more experienced riders. They must also check that the rider keeps a relaxed seat, otherwise the rider will bring his or her legs too far back and end up in a perched position which puts them out of balance.

Toe circling

This exercise is conducted with the feet out of the stirrups, the rider circling the toes of both feet together, in anti-clockwise circles. It should be done slowly, while the rest of the rider's body remains relaxed.

WHEN TO USE THE EXERCISE
a. It can be used at any time as a general loosening exercise. It helps to unlock the ankles and improve the lower leg position.
b. For riders with poor coordination this exercise can be helpful, along with other exercises, to improve their ability to move different parts of their body while keeping the rest of their body in the correct position.

Fun exercises for children

"Round the world" should be done at halt with an assistant holding the pony. The rider leaves the reins on the pony's neck and takes his or her feet out of the stirrups. They then make a complete turn in the saddle. To go in a clockwise direction, they begin by lifting their left leg over the pony's neck so that they are sitting sideways, then their

Toe circling. A good exercise for loosening the ankles and for improving coordination.

right leg over the pony's hindquarters so they are facing the tail. Then the left leg over the hindquarters so they are sitting sideways again, then the right leg over the pony's neck so they are facing the front again.

"Half dismount" should also be done at halt and, again, with an assistant holding the pony. With reins on the pony's neck and feet out of the stirrups the rider swings their right leg over the pony's neck if executing the exercise on the near side. They place their right hand on the cantle and left hand on the pommel, and twist round to face the saddle, taking their weight on their hands and keeping their arms straight. Then they swing their right leg over the cantle, moving their right arm as they do so and resume their position in the saddle. The whole movement should become fluent with practice.

For both of these exercises the instructor should make sure the pony is completely familiar with the exercise so it will not take fright, and should be on hand to steady the rider if they begin to lose balance. The instructor should also make sure that the rider makes an effort to swing their legs clear of the pony and not kick it on their way round.

Points to note

1. When the rider is to work without stirrups the usual command is "Quit and cross stirrups". The stirrup leather buckle should be pulled a few centimetres away from the stirrup bar to allow the leathers to be laid flat when crossed, rather than creating a bulge of leather which will dig into the rider's leg. In case the rider needs to dismount and remount, the offside stirrup is crossed over the horse's wither first, then the near-side stirrup. This will make it easier for the rider to let down the nearside stirrup if it is needed for remounting. The stirrups should be laid gently on the horse's shoulders, and not on the saddle where they will interfere with the rider's leg position.
2. The above exercises are a selection of the most useful. There are many variations on these themes.
3. For exercises to be of use to the rider the instructor must stress that they should be carried out slowly while the rider makes every effort to keep the rest of his or her body in a good, balanced riding position.

Helpful hints on exam technique

1. If asked to give a lesson using some rider exercises to improve position, candidates often make the mistake of using every exercise they can think of, and rush through them without giving the riders reasons for their use, and without making sure they are well executed. Try to use one or two exercises and make sure you explain why you are using them and what benefit the riders should feel. Make sure the riders carry out the exercise correctly.
2. Another common mistake is to use exercises which do not necessarily relate to the rider being taught at that moment. Try to look at the rider and assess their positional problems, then choose an exercise which will help their specific problem.

6 School Figures

By working hard at riding school figures accurately, riders will improve their ability to apply the aids clearly, fluently and effectively, at the same time improving their horse's response to the aids and ability to work in a supple and active manner between leg and hand.

It is, therefore, very important that the instructor should pay particular attention to explaining how school figures should be ridden, and also makes sure that he or she follows through the work by correcting and helping pupils when they ride the figures.

Turns and circles

a. Explain to pupils that when they are riding turns and circles the horse is moving from a straight line on to a curve. The rider's aids will, therefore, need to change in a subtle manner, from both legs at the girth asking the horse to move straight forward into an even rein contact to the aids required for a circle.

b. When on the straight line, the horse's hindquarters should follow in line behind its forehand, with its hind hoof print being placed on the same line as its front hoof print. The same applies when on a circle or turn. The hind feet should follow the line and print of the front feet. The centre line of the horse's body should also follow the line of the curve. The horse, should, therefore, be uniformly bent from poll to tail, along the line of the circle or turn being ridden.

c. The rider should prepare by looking ahead along the line he or she wishes to take. The inside leg should be used on the girth to maintain forward impulsion and to encourage the horse to engage its inside hind leg so it will bend around the curve and not fall in. The outside

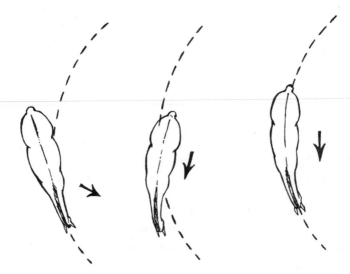

When working on a circle, the horse should be uniformly bent: (right) *from poll to tail;* (centre) *the horse falling out through its outside shoulder;* (left) *the horse swinging its quarters out.*

leg is used slightly behind the girth to help with forward impulsion and to prevent the horse swinging its quarters out. The inside rein is the guiding rein, and should gently guide the horse in the direction required, while the outside rein is the controlling rein. It controls the speed and amount of bend, so it should allow the horse to turn, but not allow it to bend its neck more than the rest of its body.

d. All the different school figures are a series of straight lines, turns, and circles, of different sizes and in different combinations. The rider needs to apply the basic aids described, making subtle changes as he or she changes direction, etc.

e. You need to make riders aware of the dimensions of the school you are working in, so they can learn to ride 20m circles, etc.

f. To ride a 20m circle in a 20mx40m area, explain to the riders that by imagining the circle divided into four quarters they will be able to ride the shape more accurately. For example, begin the circle at C on the

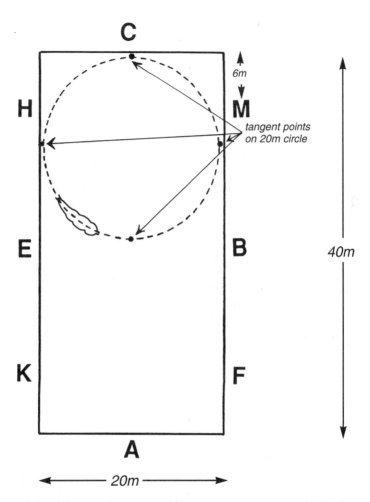

A 20m circle showing tangent points and horse uniformly bent along the line of the circle in a 20mx40m school.

right rein and ride a curve from C to a point just beyond the M marker, touching the outer track for just one stride, before curving away to the centre of the school, which is X. From X ride a curve to a point on the track just before the H marker. Take one step on the track before curving away to the C marker again. These points on the circle are referred to as the tangent points.

g. Explain to the riders that the quarter markers are situated 6m from the corners of the school. To ride an accurate 20m circle, they need to meet the outer track 10m from the corner. By aiming just a little before or beyond the quarter markers when riding a 20m circle they should end up meeting the track in the right place. If the school is marked with the tangent points of the circle, then riders can aim for these markers.

h. As the rider works through the different school movements, make sure you correct any inaccurate riding, and help him or her to understand how they can use their aids more effectively to improve the accuracy of their riding.

Points to note

1. Riders can only begin to ride accurate shapes if they are familiar with the school figures. You could demonstrate the school figures yourself, or ask an experienced rider to demonstrate them for you.
2. If you are giving the lesson in an arena with a sand surface, it is a good idea to draw the required shape in the sand. This is a particularly helpful way of showing the rider what is meant by, for example, a serpentine.

Common rider faults and problems

1. Riders often try to rely too heavily on their inside rein to direct the horse. This leads to the horse bending its neck, rather than its whole body, at the same time swinging its quarters out, and falling in onto its inside shoulder. Therefore, riders must be reminded of the need to use their inside leg more actively into the outside rein, which should be controlling the speed and bend.
2. When riding turns, the rider often underestimates the amount of preparation needed. As a result he or she overshoots the intended line. They need to be told to prepare earlier and use several half-halts to help the horse to be balanced and ready for the turn.

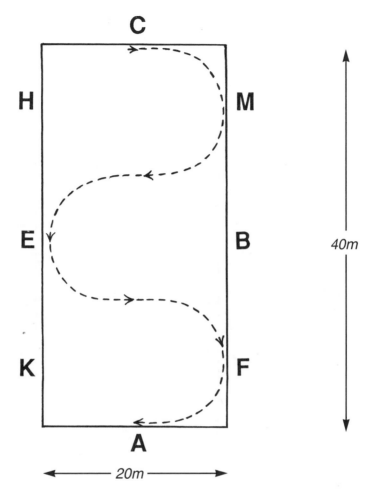

A three-loop serpentine ridden in a 20mx40m school.

3. If the rider fails to use his or her inside leg effectively, then the horse will fall-in, and lose impulsion, possibly leading to resistance and a hollow outline.
4. The rider's position often deteriorates when riding turns and circles, particularly in canter. The rider may begin to lean in and collapse their

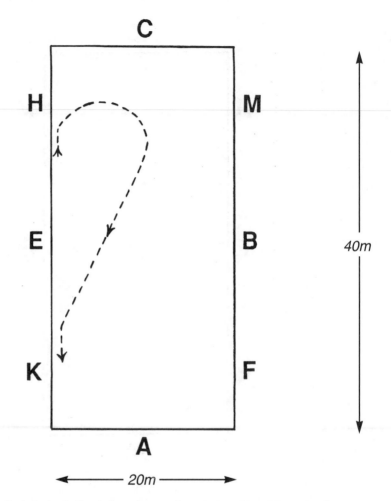

A 10m inwards half-circle (or half volte) to change the rein in a 20mx40m school.

inside hip, so their seat and weight slip to the outside. This unbalances the horse, making it difficult for it to remain straight, between leg and hand.

Helpful hints on exam technique
1. Examination candidates often make the mistake of explaining the aids

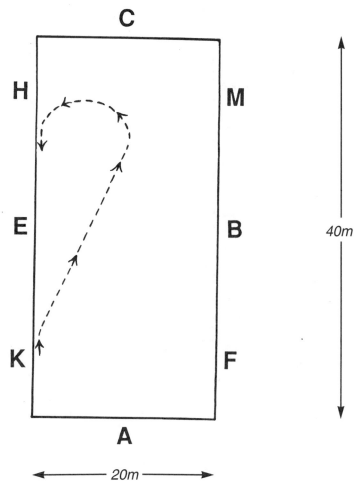

A 10m reverse half-circle (or half volte) to change the rein in a 20mx40m school.

and exercise required, but then fail to help the rider achieve a good result. You need to be observant and point out to the rider that their horse is falling-in, or that the circle has become an oblong, or that the horse is in incorrect bend. Then follow through with instructions on how to improve the problems.

2. You need to make sure that you check the rider's understanding of the

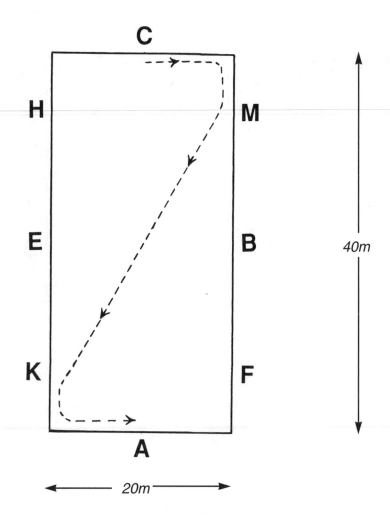

Change of rein across the long diagonal in a 20mx40m school.

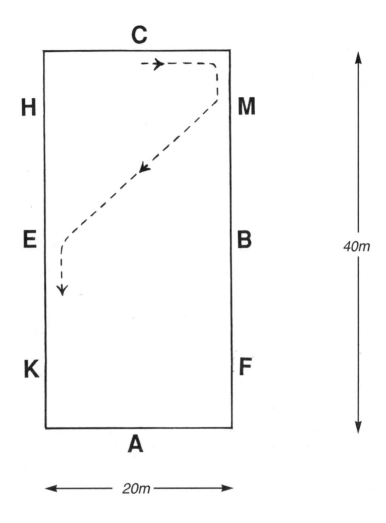

Change of rein across the short diagonal in a 20mx40m school.

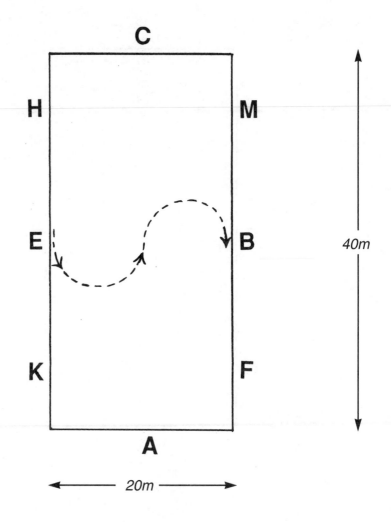

Two 10m half-circles to change the rein in a 20mx40m school.

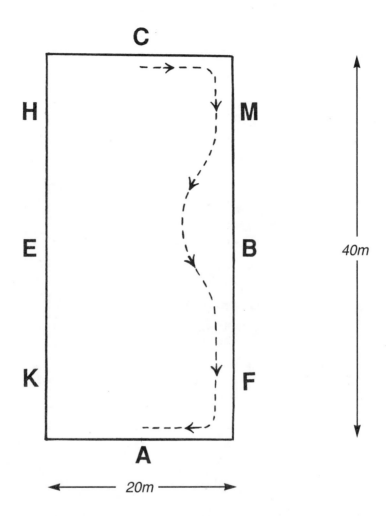

Shallow loop, 5m from track in a 20mx40m school.

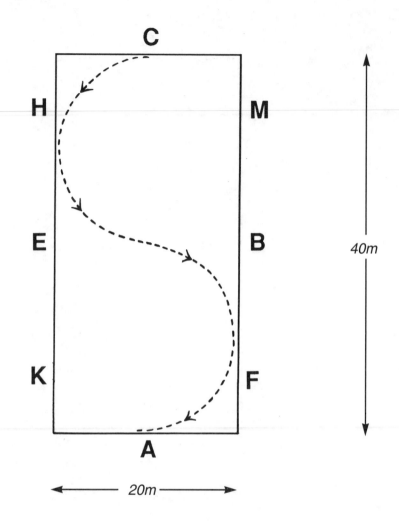

Two 20m half-circles to change the rein in a 20mx40m school.

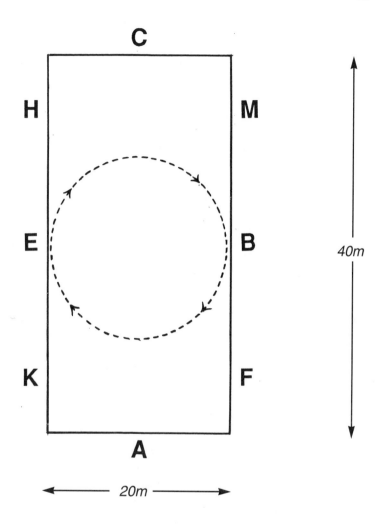

A 20m circle from **E** *or* **B** *in a 20mx40m school.*

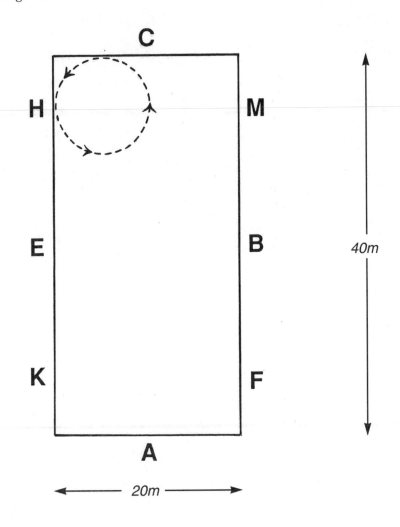

A 10m circle in a 20mx40m school.

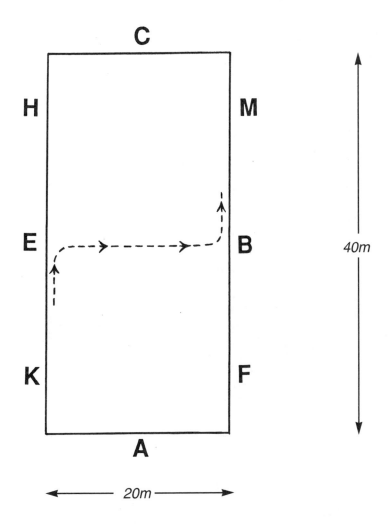

*A turn from **E** to **B** to change the rein in a 20x40m school.*

aids. Candidates often explain the exercise they would like to see, but do not check that the rider is applying the correct aids. As a result the rider is not given any help on how to improve on mistakes they are making.

7 Subjects to Cover as a Beginner Becomes a Competent Novice

Balance

a. Begin by explaining to the riders that without a rider on the horse's back, the horse will develop its own natural balance as it matures, just like a human child. However, by putting a rider on the horse, we upset its balance to a certain extent and it needs to learn how to adjust. Just like ourselves, if we were to give someone a "piggy back".

b. The horse's balance problems are added to when a rider is learning and frequently losing and changing balance. It is essential, therefore, that riders work on gaining a correct balanced position in the saddle so the horse can carry out its task.

c. For the rider to be balanced he or she needs to be sitting in the centre of the saddle with ears, shoulders, hips and heels in a vertical line. The instructor should ensure that the rider's weight is evenly distributed on their two seat bones and that they are straight when viewed from behind, not tipped to either side. In this position they should be over the horse's centre of gravity and in the best possible place for the horse to carry them smoothly.

d. The horse then needs to be encouraged to bring its hindquarters more actively under its body to support its rider, rather than letting all its weight drop on to its forehand. With too much weight on the forehand the horse becomes downhill and heavy to ride and will be difficult to manoeuvre. It also becomes strong in response to the rein aids and will be inclined to rush or, at the other extreme, be very idle. This, in turn, will make it difficult for the rider to progress with the horse.

e. Improvement of horse and rider balance is an ongoing task, but could be used on some occasions as the main theme of the lesson to heighten rider awareness. Put the rider through transitions, school movements, and changes of rein correcting positional – and horse – problems as they arise. Point out when balance is lost and help pupils to correct themselves and their horse.

f. Loss of balance will show itself in the rider whenever he or she loses position. Gripping up with the knees, tipping forward, getting left behind, lower legs slipping forwards – all are signs of loss of balance. You should point out the problem to the rider and help them to place themselves in a correct position, and therefore in balance.

g. Loss of balance in the horse shows itself when the horse is very on its forehand, hindquarters are not engaged, falling-in and rushing around turns and circles, falling into downwards transitions, etc. You should make sure the rider is aware of what is happening and help them to rectify the problem by encouraging more effective use of the leg aids into a good rein contact.

Rhythm and tempo

a. Explain to the rider that rhythm is the regularity of the footfalls in each pace, and tempo is the speed of the footfalls.

b. The rider should aim for a regular rhythm in all paces and a regular steady tempo.

c. To help riders develop feel for regular rhythmical paces, get them to practise counting out loud the beat of each pace, saying "One, two, three, four" in time with the footfalls at walk, and "One, two" in time with the footfalls in trot, and "One, two, three" in time with the foot-falls in canter. You should help them to count in time with the horse's footfalls and encourage them to ride the horse from leg into hand to keep regular gaits.

d. Another exercise could involve the use of trotting poles. As the horse's trot steps become more elevated over the poles it can make it easier for the rider to feel the rhythm and notice if it or the tempo changes each time they ride over the poles. You should tell the pupil when the rhythm and tempo change and explain how to ride the horse to keep them the same.

e. Corrections may include comments about the rider's balance as this will effect the rhythm and tempo, the accuracy with which they have ridden the movement, the way they have applied their leg and rein aids, and so on.

Impulsion

a. Explain that impulsion is the spring and activity within each gait, and should not be confused with the speed of the gait.

b. For example, a horse can go fast forward in trot or canter but the gait may be very flat so the horse has little spring. A fast, flat, trot with no impulsion will make it difficult for the horse to make a good transition to canter. A flat lethargic canter with no impulsion will lead to the horse falling into an unbalanced trot.

c. Therefore, the rider needs to encourage the horse, through effective use of their leg aids into the rein contact, to bring its hindquarters underneath its body with spring and energy so each gait has impulsion.

d. With impulsion the horse can make good transitions, feel light and fluent in its gaits, and jump well, etc.

e. By using exercises which involve plenty of transitions and changes of rein you can help the rider to be aware of gaits lacking in impulsion, and when they have managed to achieve a greater degree of impulsion.

f. If the horse runs in trot explain to the rider that it was partly due to a lack of impulsion and help him or her to ride the horse more effectively to produce a better trot. Likewise, if the horse "dribbles" from trot into an idle walk, leaning on the rider's hands, this would be partly due to a lack of impulsion in the trot. By not riding the horse's hindquarters sufficiently underneath it during the transition, impulsion is lost, and along with other rider problems a poor transition is made.

Half-halt

a. Many different phrases can be used to try and explain the half-halt, as it is very much a subtle communication between horse and rider. I like to explain it as an aid which steadies the horse and asks it to pay a little extra attention at a given moment.

b. The half-halt can vary in degree from the slightest and subtlest of aids to a more obvious visible aid, depending on whether the horse just needs a little reminder to take care, or a major check to regain completely lost attention.

c. The rider should stretch up a little in the saddle, keep their seat deep, take a slightly more restraining contact on the rein and close their legs around the horse a little more firmly. All these actions should take place simultaneously and last for just a moment.

d. The aim of the half-halt is to lighten the forehand by bringing the hindquarters more underneath the horse's body, thereby improving the horse's balance and ability to carry out the movement with ease and impulsion.

e. Riders must understand that if they prolong the half-halt it is likely to result in resistance, and cause the horse to fall onto its forehand, and therefore defeat the purpose of the exercise. It should be a quick, light, moment of communication between horse and rider.

f. To help the rider begin to use the half-halt, work them through turns and circles, asking them to try and apply the half-halt to prepare the horse for turns, and re-balance the horse after a turn. Transitions can also be used, with the rider trying to apply the half-halt to prepare for each transition.

Transitions

a. Transitions can be progressive: for example, from canter to trot to walk, or direct from canter to walk, depending on how advanced the horse and rider are.

b. When riding from walk to trot, the horse brings itself into a shorter outline, so the rider needs to shorten the reins a little in order to maintain a contact. The rider also needs to think ahead to communicate his or her wishes smoothly to the horse.

c. For an upwards transition (moving from a slower gait to a faster gait), the rider should apply forwards driving aids with both legs, while adjusting the length of the reins. As the horse changes gait, the rider should allow their hands to move with the horse so it is not restricted, but should maintain a contact to keep the horse between leg and hand.

d. For a downwards transition (moving from a faster gait to a slower gait), the rider should check their position and keep their legs riding the horse forward while softly restraining with their hands and upper body.

e. Common mistakes include the rider ceasing to use his or her legs in a downwards transition, and using too much rein which causes the horse to fall on its forehand and thus into a downwards transition in an unbalanced manner. Or, the rider uses active forwards driving aids for an upwards transition, but fails to maintain a contact so the horse rushes forward on its forehand becoming more resistant. Or the rider fails to prepare the horse for either upwards or downwards transitions, which leads to resistance and a lack of response from the horse.

f. Progressive transitions can be used throughout the lesson. You should be helping the rider to prepare for transitions so they can feel the difference between when they ride the transition well and when they don't.

Suppleness

a. Being supple is relevant to both horse and rider. When supple, you are able to move, bend and turn, with any part of your body, easily and smoothly, as well as being able to move each part of your body independently of the other. This is obviously of great advantage to both horse and rider, as it will make every exercise ridden that much easier to perform.

b. If horse and rider are stiff rather than supple, they will find it difficult to move and bend for some exercises. The rider may also find it difficult to use his or her legs independently, without moving the hands at the same time. The rider, of course, is able to say that they are finding something difficult, but the horse can only show its difficulty through resistance, loss of balance, rhythm and tempo.

c. Trying to force your body to move in a certain way, when the muscles, tendons and ligaments are reluctant to move, causes pain and may cause damage. This applies to horse and human.

d. The body needs to be made more supple through gently trying to move and stretch the stiff areas, so the muscles, tendons and ligaments are able to gradually adjust, and become more supple.

e. Most horses are easier to ride on one rein than they are on the other, which is usually one of the first things a rider notices about a horse. This is basically because the horse is more supple on one rein than the other. When working on its "stiff" rein, the rider should be made aware of helping the horse to improve, and be careful not to force it.

f. Use simple exercises like turns and circles and school figures to help the horse to become more supple.

g. To make the rider more supple, use appropriate physical exercises, and pay attention to position corrections. When the rider works on his or her position they will become more supple all the time, just through trying to move their legs, etc., into the correct place.

Forwardness

a. Phrases such as, "Send your horse forward", or "He's not really going forward", are frequently heard. It may be confusing to the rider who is trotting round a school to be told their horse is not really going forward. The horse is, of course, actually moving in a forwards direction, but to an experienced instructor or rider it may be apparent that the horse is reluctant and lacking in a real desire to go forward.

b. Instilling in the horse a desire to go forward is the key to the majority of work carried out when schooling. If the horse is reluctant, it will hang back and make it difficult for the rider to ride the horse's hindquarters under its body.

c. A horse not really going forward is seen in many different situations. It may just be idle and be making a minimum of effort. It may be finding a particular exercise difficult, and therefore be hanging back in its reluctance to work harder. It may not be sufficiently balanced to cope with a given exercise, and so on.

d. You should make riders aware of any horse lacking a desire to go forward, and help them to correct the horse through correct and effective application of the aids. Choose active exercises to help them, like canter work and plenty of transitions. If successful, the rider should feel the difference when the horse is happy to go forward. As the instructor, you need to check that the rider can feel and understand the difference.

Outline

a. From the beginning you should try to help the rider to understand what is meant by the horse being in a "good, rounded outline", and explain what is meant by the horse being "hollow".

b. When the horse's hind legs are trailing behind it, and its head is held high, or its neck is outstretched with a "poking" nose, then its back is hollow and it will have difficulty in carrying the rider. This, in turn, leads to resistance and an uncomfortable time for the rider, who will also find it difficult to communicate their wishes to the horse.

c. To help the rider picture the problems, they can imagine themselves on all fours, raising their head and hollowing their back. Add to that picture someone sitting on their back and they will soon agree that this would be very uncomfortable.

d. If, however, they imagine being on all fours with their head lowered, back raised and rounded, with their legs well under their body, they will soon agree they could take someone sitting on their back far more easily in this position.

e. A horse in a good, rounded, outline is one which has its hind legs well engaged under its body. Its forehand is light and raised. Its neck is

Imagine being on all fours with (left) your head raised and your back hollowed or (right) with your head lowered and your back rounded.

A horse working in a hollow form.

A horse working in a good outline.

arched with a flexed poll, so its head is carried with the front of its face slightly in front of the vertical. As a result of all this, it is able to stretch and round its back.

f. In this outline the horse can carry the rider with ease. Along with all the other points mentioned above, the horse will be able to work without resistance and perform any exercises asked of it.

g. If the pupil is shown a horse working in a good outline, and one that is working in a hollow form, they are bound to see that the good outline looks more comfortable and practical for both horse and rider.

h. Explain to the pupil that many riding hours will be needed to master the art of riding the horse into a good outline. Try to help them feel when the horse is beginning to work in the right way, so that they leave the lesson having achieved something. Also tell them when they are making it difficult for the horse to work in the right way, and help them to correct themselves.

i. More experienced riders should be able to begin riding their horses in a good outline, but will also need you to help them feel when they are making difficulties for their horse. This might be brought about on their part by their lack of coordination, balance, poor application of the aids, and so on.

The first steps of lateral work

Turn on the forehand

a. Explain to the rider that this is a movement in which the horse is asked to move its hindquarters in an arc, or half circle, around its forehand. Its forehand remains still, while the outside foreleg steps around the inside foreleg, and the inside hind leg steps across in front of the out-side hind leg as the quarters move round. The inside foreleg is lifted and replaced on the same spot, it should not remain fixed to the floor as a pivot.

b. The horse can be asked to perform this movement from walk. The rider applies a half-halt, then asks for the movement.

c. The movement can also be ridden from a halt. If a halt is used, the rider must be well prepared for the movement, so that once he or she has made a square halt they can ask for the movement immediately. If too much time is spent in halt, the horse is likely to "switch off", resulting in a poor attempt at the movement.

d. To ride a turn on the forehand to the right, the rider should half-halt or halt with the horse in a good outline. The inside rein (right rein) is used to indicate the direction, and ask for slight flexion at the poll so the rider can just see the horse's right eye. The inside leg (right leg) is used a little behind the girth to ask the horse to move its hind quarters over. The outside rein (left rein) keeps the horse straight, and softly restrains to prevent the horse from walking forward. The outside leg (left leg)

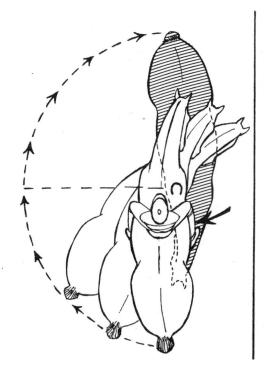

Turn on the forehand to the right. The arrow shows the direction of movement. The shaded area is the horse now that it has completed the turn.

remains on the girth and reminds the horse to keep thinking forward, and should be used to prevent the horse from stepping backwards if it tries to do so.

e. When the inside leg is used to move the quarters over, the position of the leg depends upon the response of the horse. Well educated, responsive, horses will move over when pressure is applied at the girth. Most horses of a more novice rider level will move over more easily if the leg is moved back behind the girth applying a rather more obvious leg aid.

f. Having explained these aids to the rider, a demonstration will help to clarify the movement and the aids for the rider. Either give a mounted demonstration yourself, or stand beside a horse and rider and assist them with the aids, helping to ask the horse to perform a turn on the forehand.

g. Explain to the rider that the turn on the forehand should be asked for well away from the edge of the school. If only one or two steps are going to be made, then the horse should be ridden into the middle of the arena so it can be asked to walk straight forward out of the turn. If asking for a half-turn to change the rein, then the horse can be brought on to an inner track parallel to the boards. The rider should always ask the horse to move its quarters away from the boards. Never encourage a horse to swing its quarters out.

h. The turn on the forehand is a very good coordination exercise for the rider. It provides him or her with the chance to feel the horse stepping sideways underneath them. To ride the exercise successfully they must use each leg and hand individually, which can help them to make great improvement in their coordination.

i. There is a practical application for turn on the forehand, as it enables the rider to position their horse in a suitable way for them to be able to open a gate when mounted. There are often other situations when it is helpful to be able to move the horse's quarters over. For example, it may help you to position your horse in a gap by the side of the road in order to let a very large vehicle go past.

j. The exercise benefits the horse, as it teaches it to move away from the rider's leg. Also, as the horse is asked to step across with its inside hind leg, bringing it further under its body, it will supple the horse and bring its hindquarters more underneath it, providing the movement is well executed.

k. As the turn on the forehand is a quiet and fairly stationary movement, it is the easiest way for a rider to learn to coordinate the aids and feel the lateral movement at the same time. The rider can take each step at a time, riding the horse forward and straight out of the movement should coordination be lost and they need to reorganise themselves. When they have mastered the aids, and can apply them well, they can use the turn on the forehand as a means of changing the rein, by asking the horse to continue the movement until it is completely facing the opposite way to which it started.

Points to note

1. If riders are making a turn on the forehand to change the rein, they

should be told to change their whips into their outside hand before they begin the turn. In this way the whip can be used to back up the leg aid asking the horse to move over, and will also be in the correct hand to continue riding forward with, once the change of rein is completed.

2. Riders should always be told to ride their horses actively forward after the turn on the forehand movement, either in an active walk, trot, or for more experienced riders, canter. This is to ensure that the horse will continue to think forward. If the turn has not been well ridden the horse may have begun to step backwards and forward activity must be re-established. If the turn is well ridden, the engagement of the hind quarters should be put to good use.

3. Whenever possible, make sure the rider is riding a schoolmaster horse when being taught a new movement. For example, if the rider is trying to understand and use aids for the first time, he or she needs a horse that will help them by performing the movement if they "press the right buttons". If the movement is new to the horse as well, you have a recipe for confusion and frustration.

Common rider faults and problems

1. Riders often forget the need to begin the turn from a square halt, and find their horse stepping backwards as a result. This is a very bad fault, as it will only serve to put the horse on its forehand, with its hind legs not engaged. The same problem will occur if the horse is half-halted whilst in a sloppy and inactive walk.

2. If the rider is disorganised before they start the turn, they often begin using incorrect aids and then change them part way through, obviously causing great confusion for the horse.

3. Riders try to use too much inside rein which causes the horse to bend its neck and begin walking a small circle, rather than moving its quarters over.

4. If the rider fails to use their outside rein, the horse will fall out through its outside shoulder and end up making a sort of turn about its middle.

5. Riders are frequently seen with their outside leg sticking out away from the horse's side, as they have completely forgotten the need to use this leg. As a result, the horse begins to step back.

6. The rider may also look down and collapse towards their inside leg, leading to a complete loss of position and balance which will make it very difficult for the horse to make the turn.

Leg-yielding

a. Explain to the rider that this is a lateral movement in which the horse is asked to move both forwards and sideways at the same time. The horse's inside fore and hind legs will cross over and in front of the outside fore and hind.

b. The movement can be ridden in walk or trot. The horse should remain in a good outline, in an active gait, and take even strides. Its body should remain straight, and it should have a very slight bend at the poll so that it is looking away from the direction of the movement.

c. Riders will benefit from a demonstration of the movement at this point, so they can picture what they will be asking their horses to do. You can

Leg-yielding to the right in trot.

either ride the movement yourself, or ask an experienced rider and horse to demonstrate for you while you explain what they are doing.

d. To ask the horse to leg-yield to the left, the rider uses his or her inside leg (the right leg) on or slightly behind the girth (depending on the horse's responses), to move the horse over. The inside rein (the right rein) asks for a slight bend at the poll so the horse looks away from the direction of the movement, and the rider can just see the horse's inside eye. The outside leg (the left leg) is used at the girth to ride the horse forward and help keep it straight. The outside rein (the left rein) controls the amount of bend so helping to keep the horse straight.

e. The position of the inside leg varies from on, or a little behind, the girth depending on which part of the horse's body needs to be influenced more. If the forehand needs to be moved over more, then the leg is used at the girth. If the hindquarters need to be moved over more, then the leg is used behind the girth.

f. To begin with the rider can be asked to ride their horse around the arena to establish a good active walk, then turn and ride straight along the three-quarter line. If you position yourself at the end of the three-quarter line, you can check to see if the rider is sitting straight and riding a straight line.

g. The rider can then ride some steps of leg-yield, by riding up the three-quarter line, and then leg-yielding out towards the boards.

h. If they master the movement in walk on both reins, riders can progress to riding it in trot.

i. When first practising the leg-yield, and as the boards of the school act as a magnet to the horse, it is usually easier for riders to move from the three-quarter line to the track . As they progress, they can practise leg-yielding from the track to the three-quarter line, or in any other appropriate place in the school.

j. When riding out on a hack, a rider can practise riding leg-yield from one side of the track to the other.

k. Explain that the leg-yield movement is a good suppling exercise for the horse and a way of helping to engage its hindquarters.

l. The leg-yield helps riders' coordination, as they have to use each hand and leg individually to give slightly different aids.

m. The movement is of practical help when positioning the horse. For example, when riding out on the roads leg-yielding will help the rider to move the horse into the edge of the road to allow cars to pass.

Points to note

1. Try to use a schoolmaster horse to teach the rider about leg-yielding.
2. Once the rider has had a chance to practise a little on each rein, it is a good idea to go on riding some simple but active movements. If your pupils do this it will help you straighten up the horse and rider again, as they are bound to have fallen into the trap of collapsing themselves, allowing the horse to fall out through its outside shoulder. Explain that you will return to the leg-yield exercise later, or in another lesson, as it is not good for the horse to be asked to keep moving sideways without a break. The horse may otherwise become resistant and more difficult to ride into the movement.
3. Always emphasise that forward movement and keeping the horse straight should be rider priorities.
4. Make sure riders have achieved a good level of coordination when riding the turn on the forehand before progressing to leg-yielding. They will find leg-yielding more difficult – and if they are struggling with the turn on the forehand, they have little hope of grasping leg-yielding.

Common rider faults and problems

1. Riders often hurry into the leg-yield before making sure that their horse is straight. As a result the horse just bends its neck and falls out through its outside shoulder.
2. As with the turn on the forehand, the rider may apply the inside leg and rein aids, and completely forget the outside leg and rein which should be supporting the movement. The horse is likely to fall out through its outside shoulder, bend its neck and escape the movement.
3. If the horse is quite responsive about moving sideways, riders may find themselves asking the horse to step over and forget that the horse should also move forward.
4. Through lack of coordination, the rider may confuse the horse so it thinks it is being asked to move faster forward, and not sideways at all.

8 Pole Work and Jumping

Ground poles

a. Individual ground poles can be used to make a lesson more interesting and demanding. They give both horse and rider something to focus on, and improve horse and rider skills like balance, suppleness, and coordination.

b. Begin with one pole positioned on an inner track at the B or E marker. Explain to the rider that they are to walk their horse over the pole, aiming for the centre, working for an active walk to encourage the horse to pick up its feet.

c. Make sure the rider realises that the aims of the exercise are: to test their ability to ride their horse between leg and hand in a straight line; to help them feel when the horse is in a balanced and active walk; to help the horse become more supple as it has to lift and flex its joints more; to test both horse and rider's ability to maintain balance when negotiating an object.

d. You can go on to place one or two more poles around the school, perhaps on an inner track or along the centre line, so the rider can work over the poles when turning across the school. Adding more poles tests and improves all the above points to a greater degree, as well as making horse and rider think ahead and plan more as they have to constantly be on the look out for poles.

e. Go on to work over the poles in trot, use transitions, and use different school figures that incorporate the poles. For example: turns across the school, turns across the diagonals, serpentines, etc.

f. If the horse knocks a pole, help the rider to understand whether it was

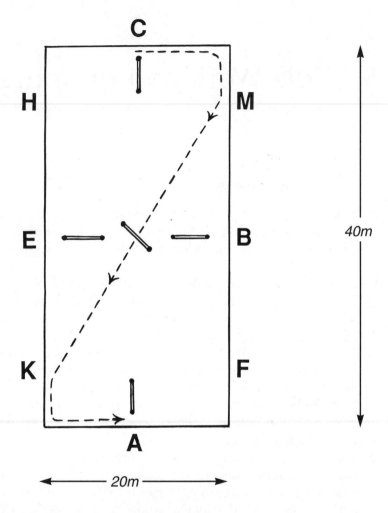

Single poles can be placed in various places around the school to make exercises more interesting, varied and demanding. Position poles that can be included in the riding of school figures. Here, for example, a turn across the diagonal . . .

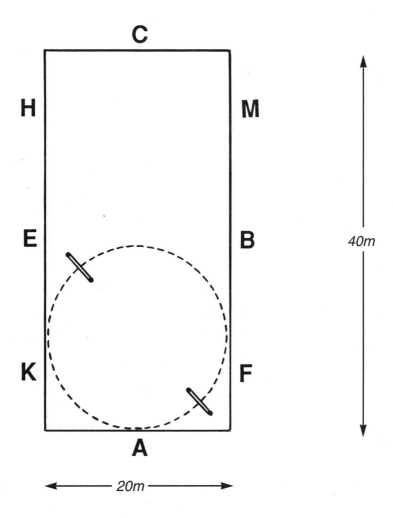

. . . or when riding a 20m circle . . .

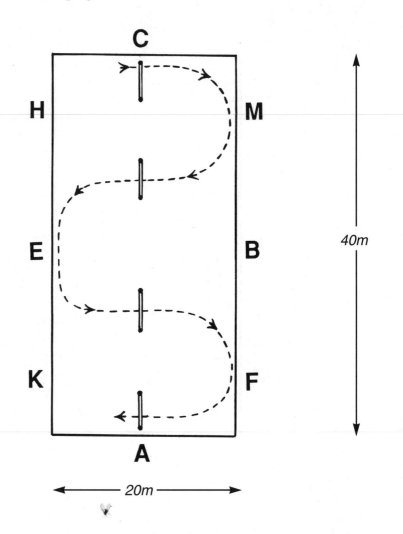

. . . or a three-loop serpentine.

because the trot or walk was too fast, slow, inactive, etc. Go on to help pupils correct the gait, and pay attention to the way they are riding the school figures.

g. Give plenty of praise when pupils ride well, but don't say "Good" if the horse is knocking poles and falling-in around turns. Riders need help from you to distinguish between when they have a good gait, with the horse between leg and hand, and when they have not.

Points to note

1. Pole work can tell you a great deal about the amount of progress a rider has made. He or she may appear to be able to ride their horse in a regular gait around a circle or particular school figure, but when you put one or two poles in their path it becomes apparent that they are finding it difficult to be accurate and that they are not really in complete control of their horse as yet.

2. Using poles can make school work more interesting, especially during periods of bad weather when you may be confined to lessons in the school week after week. During good weather you can probably create variety in lessons by riding in a field, doing some cross-country riding, as well as school work. When you are restricted to the school, poles can be used.

Common rider faults and problems

1. Riders often find it difficult to aim to the centre of the pole. If the horse is drawn towards the outer track and the rider does not use his or her outside leg the result is that the horse nearly misses the pole. This is a good time to point out to the rider how important it is to use both legs.

2. There is a tendency for riders to look down at the poles. They should be encouraged to look up, otherwise they will lose balance and put the horse on its forehand.

3. If the horse knocks one pole, the rider may ride the horse into a faster gait and mistake speed for impulsion. The horse is likely to go on

knocking poles as a result. Try to make it clear to pupils that they need to ask for a more active gait, not just speed.

Trotting poles

a. When horse and rider are working well over individual ground poles, you can progress to trotting poles.
b. These should be placed 1.4m–1.5m apart for an average horse. It will be necessary to shorten the distance a little for ponies and lengthen the distance a little for larger, long-striding horses.
c. Having introduced the horse and rider to a single pole first, two more poles can be added, placed the appropriate distance apart, to make a line of three. It is not advisable to use two poles, trotting distance apart, as they can be misunderstood by the horse and it may attempt to jump them.
d. Before laying out poles, instructors should measure their normal stride length, against a tape laid on the ground. Once you know your stride length (for most people it is close to 1m in length) it will be easy to lay out poles the correct distance apart.
e. You should place one pole on the ground, then stand with your heels against the pole. Take one stride away from the pole, then place one foot in front of the foot that has completed the stride. Now place the next pole at the end of your toes. You should find this is close to the correct distance for trotting poles. You could measure the distance, then you will know if this way of setting out the poles is right for you. Repeat the process to position the next pole.
f. At a later stage, more experienced riders could be given more poles to work over. To discourage horses from jumping, an odd number of poles is usually used. Do not use more than three poles before horse and rider have really established their balance and rhythm.
g. If the poles are the correct distance apart for the horse's stride length, it will place first one fore foot, then the other, right in the middle of the space between each pole. If it is working actively and tracking up, then the hind foot will follow into the print of the forefoot. You need to practise watching horses and riders working over trotting poles in order to

develop an eye for whether the poles are well placed, or whether the rider is not riding the horse well over the poles. If the horse has problems with the poles, you need to be able to see if it is because the poles need adjusting, or the rider needs correction.

h. Trotting poles should improve the rider's balance, help him or her to feel the horse's trot steps, and improve their coordination. Using the poles should, therefore, improve their ability both to ride their horses into an active balanced trot and to feel when they have achieved a good gait.

i. Trotting poles will also help the horse's balance, improve its rhythm, and make the horse more supple as it has to lift and flex its joints more.

j. Make sure the rider realises that the horse should remain in a good outline when working over poles, and that it will help the horse to become more supple if it is allowed to stretch a little and look down at the poles.

k. Tell riders to keep an elastic contact with the reins, and to follow the horse with their hands as it stretches, without losing the rein contact.

l. Once horse and rider have ridden over the poles two or three times from each direction, it is a good idea to move on to another exercise. For example, explain to the pupil that trotting pole work has improved the way the horse is going, so you are now going on to a canter exercise. Your purpose here is to see if the improved trot work can also help improve the canter transitions. Or, you could explain that you are going on to a canter exercise to see if it will help improve the trot work, by making the horse more supple and active. You could then work the horse and rider over the trotting poles again and see if the pole work has improved, as a result.

m. Always try to put each exercise to good use. Try not to get stuck on one exercise improving one point in an isolated way. Each exercise should be linked to improving the horse and rider combination as a whole.

Points to note

1. Where you position the poles will make the exercise more or less demanding. Putting the poles at the B or E marker on the long side of the arena creates a fairly straightforward exercise. If the poles were

placed across the width of the school, the riders would have a shorter approach and getaway line which would make the exercise more demanding. They would have to ride more accurately and maintain an active gait while turning and then straightening the horse. Again, variation of this sort is a simple way of making a lesson more interesting.

2. Do not ask riders to walk over trotting poles. They are not the correct distance for the horse and will cause it to lose balance and stumble. If you would like to build up to trotting poles by using walk first, the poles must be placed closer together. Approximately 1m apart should be the right distance for walking poles. Alternatively, walk over one ground pole, then trot over a single pole, then progress to the three trotting poles. Schoolmaster horses will be familiar with the exercise, and this would be a progressive way of working up to trotting poles without plunging pupils into them straight away.

3. Make sure you are prepared to re-position the poles if they are knocked out of place, and if they do not appear to be the right distance for the horse.

4. Riders should rise to the trot when working over trotting poles, to leave the horse's back free to move. Alternatively, they could adopt a forward position as preparation for jumping.

5. I do not recommend using trotting poles in front of a jump for novice riders. Some horses see the fence beyond the poles and begin to rush, leading to them jumping or stumbling over the poles. The poles are then a hindrance and not a help. If they are used for more experienced riders, then there should be a distance of approximately 3m between the last pole and the jump.

Common rider faults and problems

1. Riders may approach the trotting poles with a fast, flat, trot in their effort to gain an energetic gait. As a result the horse runs through the poles and knocks them. You must tell pupils why the horse knocked the poles and try to help them establish more impulsion and a steadier gait.

2. The rider may make a poor approach to the poles so the horse does not

meet them straight and cannot keep a good gait and rhythm working over them. It may help if a cone is placed for the riders to ride around before they approach the poles.

3. The rider will often look down at the poles, causing loss of position and therefore balance.
4. Some riders are so intent on looking at the poles that they forget to use their legs. The result is that the horse gradually slows to a walk as it approaches the poles.

Introducing jumping

a. Begin by explaining to the rider the need to adopt a different position, in order to stay in balance with the horse, when jumping. The horse needs the rider to take his or her weight off its back so it is more free to round itself over the fence, and lift its limbs clear of the poles. At the same time the horse will stretch its head and neck forward. The rider needs to be able to follow this movement with the rein contact in order not to restrict the horse. Throughout the jump, the horse's centre of gravity and balance is changing. The rider, therefore, needs to adopt a fluent position that changes with the horse.

b. The position required is achieved by the rider taking the stirrups up to a shorter length. The number of holes will vary according to the stirrup leathers themselves, and how deep the seat of the rider is when riding on the flat. These factors make a difference to how long riders have their stirrups for dressage work. Usually two or three holes will be about right.

c. While the horse is standing still, the rider should be shown the basic forward position they need to adopt for jumping. This will give them a chance to feel how the position needs to change, and the different muscles, suppleness, and balance that will be required. Tell the rider to lift his or her seat out of the saddle, and push it out behind them towards the back of the saddle. At the same time they should fold their body at the hip joints, keeping their back flat, while bringing their shoulders down towards the horse's neck. Their lower leg must remain

The basic forward position: the rider is moving her seat back and folding her upper body down and forward.

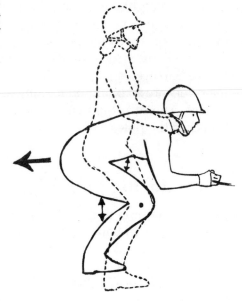

Out of balance. Here, the rider has tipped forward because she has not moved her seat back.

underneath them, with the heels down. If they have found the correct balance, they should now be able to stretch their arms forward with their hands reaching towards the bit, and not lose balance.

d. A demonstration of this forward position will be invaluable at this point, along with your help to put the rider into the correct position.

e. Riders now need to practise this position when riding around the school, first at walk, then trot and eventually canter. They also need to practise using their leg aids with their stirrups at the shorter jumping length.

f. This work is very tiring for most riders and should only be gradually introduced, just spending a few minutes of each lesson on forward position to begin with. It can be incorporated with the ground pole exercises, telling the riders to imagine that the poles are jumps. This will help prepare them in a progressive manner for their first jumping experience.

g. As the rider becomes accustomed to this position he or she can be introduced to the five, or seven, phases of jumping. Approach, take off, flight, landing and getaway, are the main five. The turn into the fence and the turn away can be added to make seven.

h. Using individual ground poles, and trotting poles, put the riders through the various exercises which incorporate practice of forward position and the phases of jumping.

i. Explain the importance of a good turn into the fence. The turn must be accurate in order that the horse be presented straight at the fence with the best possible chance of seeing it and jumping it well. It must also be an active turn, with the horse kept securely between leg and hand. This also applies to the turn after the fence, as this will be the primary preparation for the next fence when jumping a course.

j. The approach must be straight, active and positive, whether in trot or canter. The horse should not be rushed or interfered with. The rider must remain in balance, and keep the horse between leg and hand, whilst keeping the seat light in preparation for the take off. They must not tip forward and lose balance.

k. The take off should be balanced and flowing, with horse and rider moving together in balance. The horse should take off at an appropriate

When jumping, the rider should adopt a position that changes fluently with the horse.

distance from the fence to allow for a good "clean" jump. If the horse stands off the fence or gets too close, this will generally be due to the turn and approach not having being well ridden.

l. In flight over the fence the horse should keep a good round outline, termed the "bascule". The rider must remain in balance and not restrict or hinder the horse in any way. The rider's position should flow through a series of changes, from following the horse forward as it reaches the highest part of its jump, then levelling out, then gradually sitting up again as the horse begins its descent, so their weight is not thrown onto the horse's forehand as it lands.

m. On landing, the rider's seat should not return heavily to the saddle, but remain light and balanced over the horse's centre of gravity, while the horse re-balances itself and brings its hindquarters underneath it again.

n. The getaway should be calm and purposeful, with the rider encouraging the horse to engage an active and balanced gait again, without rushing it, so it is re-balanced and prepared for the next fence. Attention should be paid to the leading leg in canter, to make sure the horse is balanced for the direction in which the rider wishes it to go.

o. The rider can begin practising all of the above points to some extent, while working over the poles. These can be placed between jump wings or blocks to give the rider more of a feel of approaching a jump. Tell the rider to assume a forward position over the ground poles, then to sit up again and ride away and prepare for the next pole.

p. When you feel the rider is ready, introduce the first jump. This could be a very low cross-pole, approximately 20–30cm high at its centre. Do not use any trotting poles or placing poles on the approach, as at this stage they will only create more problems for the rider. Although a cross-pole usually attracts a horse to its centre, at this very low height, and with schoolmaster horses, you may prefer to use a straight bar fence as the rider may have difficulty in approaching straight and end up presenting the horse to one side of the fence. If it is a cross-fence, the horse will be jumping a slightly higher part of the fence, which will not happen if you use a straight bar. You can use either type of fence, but be prepared to make changes to the fence according to how the rider copes.

q. Make sure you have positioned the jump where it is easy to approach and ride away from, and use cones to give the rider a fixed point to ride around on approach and getaway.

r. Provided the horse you are using is well behaved (and it should be for a first jumping lesson), there should not be any need to place the jump against the wall to prevent the horse from running out. It is easier to leave the track clear, so the rider can use the whole school to establish a good active approach gait.

s. To begin with, tell the rider to approach in trot but, to make sure the rider does not interfere with the horse, explain that if the horse does begin to canter the rider should not worry. They must allow the horse to continue and then concentrate on riding to the fence and following the horse as it jumps. Many schoolmaster horses will take one or two steps of canter just prior to the jump.

t. Riders should be told to hold a neck strap or the horse's mane, as well as the reins, in order not to be left behind, and to prevent them catching hold of the horse's mouth for balance. Therefore, it is best if the rider approaches in a forward position so he or she is well prepared when they reach the jump.

u. Give the rider plenty of encouragement and praise where it is due, then explain where they made mistakes and help them to repeat the exercise showing improvement.

Points to note

1. Take care not to move on to higher fences or anything more difficult too quickly. It is important to establish balance, coordination, suppleness, etc., and therefore rider confidence. To prevent the problem of the horse anticipating the jump, move on to another jump of the same type, but in a different place in the school.

2. It is generally better to position jumps and poles off the outer track. It is easier to help the rider establish a good gait, or the correct canter lead, and so on, if the outer track is free. Otherwise the rider is faced with avoiding the jumps, as well as trying to concentrate on the areas you are trying to work on. If you have a very large school to work in, this may not apply.

3. Make sure you structure and plan your lesson to include plenty of

working-in time, with the riders using the shorter stirrup length, and keeping in mind that it will be tiring for once a week riders who will need plenty of short rests.

Common rider faults and problems

1. Riders are often so intent on the jump that they forget to use their legs, which results in the horse slowing to a walk and stopping when it gets to the jump. This is one of the reasons for not using a placing pole at this stage, as it is likely to bring the horse to a walk even earlier.
2. The rider may lean too far forward and be in front of the movement, so they take off before the horse and completely lose balance over the jump. This could lead to a fall on landing.
3. A nervous rider, or one lacking suppleness, is likely to get left behind and not be able to follow the horse, resulting in loss of balance. They are also likely to bump down on the horse's back, and/or pull on its mouth, which will not help to encourage the horse to jump again.
4. Despite practice in forward position, some riders will stand up over the jump, instead of folding forward. Again they are unable to follow the horse smoothly in this position.
5. The rider will often forget everything they have been told about the approach, resulting in poor presentation at the jump, so the horse jumps awkwardly, making it very difficult for the rider to follow.
6. Riders often put all their energy and concentration into approaching and jumping the fence, then collapse in relief on landing. This sometimes leads to the horse stopping quickly, or turning sharply, which can lead to a fall for the rider.

Placing poles

a. When the riders have had plenty of practice jumping single fences, and they have reached a reasonable standard of proficiency, it may be helpful to them if they are introduced to a placing pole in front of the fence.
b. Provided that they approach in an active gait the pole will help the horse to take off at the right place in front of the fence. The rider can

develop a feel for a good take off point and know when the horse is going to jump. This helps them to flow with the horse and develop feel and balance, etc.

c. A placing pole should be positioned approximately 3m from the fence. Make the distance a little shorter for ponies, or if the rider is approaching in trot. Provided that you have measured your stride length, you can lay out the pole by standing with your back to the jump, then take three strides away from the fence and place the pole at the end of your last step. If you know your strides are short or long, then you can adjust accordingly.

d. Be careful about using placing poles if working with a novice rider and a horse you do not know. Some very onward-bound and long-striding horses may try to jump the pole and jump all in one, which could lead to an accident or loss of confidence for horse and rider.

Grid work

a. Building up a grid of fences is a good way of building rider confidence, improving suppleness, feel for stride and rhythm, and balance. It also helps to keep the horse supple, make it more athletic, and help it to develop greater balance and rhythm with its rider.

b. As the instructor, you are responsible for building a grid that will help the horse and rider. It is vital that you place each fence at the correct distance apart. If you don't, then you will make the exercise more difficult for the horse and rider and destroy their confidence, rather than help with any of the above points.

c. To progress from a placing pole into a single fence, add a second fence to the line approximately 6.5m–7m away. This distance allows the horse to take one stride of canter between the two fences before taking off to jump the second fence. This single stride of canter between two fences is often referred to as "one non-jumping stride".

d. If the rider copes well with these fences you can add a third fence to the line which could also be 6.5m–7m away.

e. At this stage keep each fence as a simple cross-pole or small upright. If the rider progresses to coping well with this line of fences, you could make the last fence into a small spread.

f. You can go on to vary the number of fences in the grid. A combination of different distances could also include two fences with "two non-jumping strides" between them. For the horse to take these two canter strides between two fences, you need a distance of approximately 10m–11m. Bearing in mind that novice riders are likely to lose impulsion throughout the grid, it is usually better to keep to slightly shorter distances. To set out these fences, you would need to take about ten or eleven of your own strides between the two fences.

Points to note

1. If riders are jumping from trot, keep the distances between fences a little shorter, as the horse will not cover as much ground as it would if cantering into a fence. Likewise, horses tend to be more forward going when jumping outside, especially if in a field, so distances can be a little longer outside and shorter inside. Ponies generally need shorter distances, but some short-striding horses, especially those that may be used for first jumping lessons, need quite short distances too.

2. You need to develop a feel for the right distance through practice. Helping an experienced instructor who is giving jumping lessons is a good way of gaining experience; you can lay out the poles and jumps, and they can check and help you with the distances.

3. It will take you several lessons, at least, to practise and build up to jumping a grid. For some pupils reaching this stage may take a long time, especially if they have any problems with confidence. Encourage them to "have a go", but never push them into attempting something they are not ready for. Apart from causing accident and injury, you could ruin their enjoyment of jumping for ever. There is a great deal of responsibility resting on the shoulders of an instructor; a responsibility which should never be taken lightly.

Common rider faults and problems

1. Riders may cease to use their legs when riding through a grid. They concentrate on the jumps and their position but forget to encourage the

horse by use of their leg aids. As a result, the horse loses impulsion and may grind to a halt part way through the line of fences.

2. Many riders, through lack of suppleness and balance, fail to recover their position between fences and end up leaning further and further forward out of balance. Grid work is very useful for improving on this problem.

3. The rider may fail to approach the grid with an active gait, making it difficult for the horse to jump a row of fences as it is lacking impulsion. This highlights for the rider how important it is to have a quality gait on approach.

4. Likewise, the rider may rush the horse to the grid, causing it to flatten and knock down all the fences.

5. Any number of positional faults may be apparent. These are likely to hinder or restrict the horse. You need to point these out to the rider, and help him or her to make corrections. Riders looking down and to one side is very common. It is helpful if you stand at the end of the grid, and hold up an object, or a number of fingers, that the riders have to identify as they ride down the grid. They will have to look up in order to be able to do this.

Jumping a course of fences

a. When the riders appear to be quite proficient at jumping single fences and grids, they are now ready to go on to jumping a few fences linked together as a course.

b. This will be far more demanding on them; they will have to think about turning and changing direction, as well as jumping the fences. Also, they must think ahead more to where they are going next, and make sure the horse is well prepared for the next jump.

c. Begin by using three small, simple fences that can be jumped from both directions. Too many fences in the school will cause confusion for the rider. Place the fences where the rider will have plenty of room to approach and ride away.

d. Having gone through the usual warm-up period for jumping, work the rider over each of the fences individually, then practise linking two together, then three, then maybe four or five.

e. In previous lessons you should already have stressed to pupils the importance of riding away from the fence, working to pick up a good active gait. Explain to the riders that as soon as they are jumping one fence they should be thinking ahead to the next fence. Therefore, as they land they must ride a good line and turn, checking that the horse is on the correct canter lead, and recovering their balance and position in the saddle.

f. The riders are bound to make mistakes to begin with, and will need help and guidance in areas that need improvement. Explain to them that if they find they have lost position and balance and need time to reorganise themselves and the horse, they should ride a circle to re-establish canter on the correct leading leg, before trying to approach the next fence.

g. Point out to pupils that all the work covered in previous lessons will be needed now they are jumping a course. This includes the work on the flat, not just the work over fences. To jump the course, they need to keep a good balanced position, they need to apply the correct aids for riding turns, circles, transitions, and the half-halt, and they need to put together all the phases of jumping.

h. As the instructor you need to highlight for the riders how each of the exercises is linked to the other. This, so as to remind them not to forget all they have been taught so far and to prevent them from throwing themselves into the course without due preparation and thought throughout.

Points to note

1. When pupils are concentrating on riding a course, you should not try to say too much to them with regard to corrections. It is better to take the time to summarise their problems at the end. They are unlikely to hear everything you have to say while they are trying to ride the course, so confine your comments to the most important points, such as: telling them to make a circle; saying where the next fence is if they have lost their way; telling them to trot and change their canter lead;

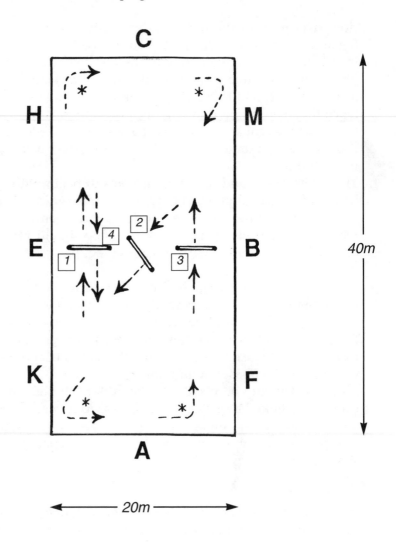

Set out a simple plan of just two or three jumps, beginning by placing the poles on the ground, so that the riders can trot around the course before the jumps are built. Here, three fences can be approached from each side to make a course of four, or more, jumps as numbered. Note: the stars indicate the position of cones, placed to help riders.

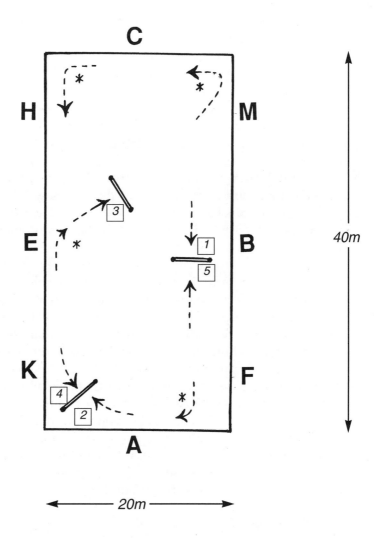

An alternative simple plan.

and so on. Making too many comments will only distract pupils when they have a lot to think about. Having made corrections at the end, you can tell them to ride the course, or part of it, again, paying particular attention to the corrections you have made. Hopefully they will then show some improvement.

2. To begin with, you can make the task easier for the riders by placing cones in appropriate places for them to ride around. This should help them to ride a good track and therefore present the horse straight at each fence.

3. Another helpful way of building up to riding a course is to lay a single pole on the ground where each of the jumps will be positioned. Put jump wings or blocks at the end of each pole. The riders can trot round the course, practise their turns, and fix the ground plan in their minds, before the jumps are put up.

4. As riders become more proficient at riding over a course, combination fences can be included. Combinations are doubles (and, for the more experienced riders, trebles) with one or two non-jumping strides between fences. Fences at related distances can also be used. A related distance is when two fences are further apart than those in a combination, but still a set number of strides apart (up to five strides). A horse's stride length is approximately equal to 3.5m–4m. Having taken eleven human strides to set out a two-stride distance, you can now add four more human strides for each horse stride required.

5. To build a course of fences quickly you need to make good use of your assistants. The best way is to place a single pole in the exact position you would like each fence to be. When all the poles are laid out and in position, your assistants can start bringing wings and jump cups to the appropriate places as you begin building fences.

Common rider faults and problems

1. The rider may be unable to cope with jumping one fence and, at the same time, be thinking ahead to the next fence. This leads to a disorganised getaway from the fence and little or no preparation for the next fence. As a result, the rider has to ride a circle after each fence and ends up riding the fences individually rather than as a course. This usually

occurs if the rider is nervous or is simply not ready to ride a course as yet.

2. After jumping one fence, the rider will often fail to regain a balanced position, resulting in an inability to ride on to the next fence with the horse between leg and hand. As a result of this, the rider's jumping, application of the aids, etc., deteriorates further as he or she tries to continue with the course.

3. If the rider is riding a forward-going horse, he or she may forget to use their leg aids to good effect and end up pulling the horse around turns, allowing it to get faster and flatter as it progresses around the course. This results in the horse falling in and getting longer and longer and the rider getting more and more out of balance.

4. Riders often think only about where the next fence is and fail to ride a good track, at the same time not giving themselves a moment to check and change the horse's canter lead if necessary.

9 The Lead Rein Lesson

When to use this type of lesson

a. Lessons on the lead rein are most frequently used when children are first learning to ride; it is the ideal way for young children as they are small, not very strong, and often uncoordinated to begin with. Using the lead rein, the instructor can keep control of the pony whilst staying in close contact with the child and is able to hold on to them if they begin to lose balance, thereby making sure that the child does not fall off at this early stage in their riding career. It is the policy of some riding schools to only take children for lessons from the age of five years upwards. At this age they are physically stronger and more able to keep their balance. If younger children are taken for lessons, a helper may be needed to hold the child steady in the saddle for any trot work. It may be necessary to ask a parent to accompany the child.

b. A very nervous adult beginner rider may prefer to be led to start with, although it is often thought that an adult rider will feel belittled on the lead rein, but this is not always the case. It can be a confidence giving way of starting an adult rider who really would like to try to learn to ride, but who becomes very nervous once on board. Leading such riders helps to eliminate the common fear that the horse may run off.

c. Many disabled riders are given lead rein lessons if their disabilities are such that they are unable to control the horse on their own. The Riding for the Disabled Association (RDA) are always looking for "helpers" who can come and lead horses as well as help support disabled riders, providing a steadying hand to keep them in balance once they are on the horse.

d. A lead rein lesson can also be given by a mounted instructor. This can be a useful way of taking quite a good child rider out on a hack. The rider might be very capable in an enclosed arena, but not able to control a pony if it decided to set off at a faster gait in open spaces.

The instructor's equipment

a. A lead rein with a coupling which can be attached to either side of the bit for good control. The lead rein needs to be strong, comfortable to hold, long enough to allow the instructor to move away from the pony at times, but not so long that it hangs in coils around the instructor's feet.
b. A stick, in case the horse or pony needs a little encouragement to walk or trot on with more enthusiasm.
c. Standard riding turnout, which includes a hard hat of (in 1997) the most up-to-date BSI (British Standards Institute) standard, currently 6473 or 4472. Also PAS 015. The instructor may need to ride the horse or pony to demonstrate a movement like rising trot, or even just to demonstrate mounting and dismounting.
d. Strong comfortable footwear that they will be able to walk and run in easily.
e. Gloves should always be worn when leading, in case the horse pulls. Without gloves a lead rope could cause a rope burn, and possibly lead to the instructor letting go of the horse or pony, which would not be a desirable situation.

The horse's or pony's equipment

a. The horse or pony should be tacked up in its usual bridle. Generally this will have a mild snaffle bit, as beginner riders are bound to make an occasional uncoordinated pull at the horse's mouth, and this type of bit is less likely to cause any damage or upset to the horse.
b. For small children the reins need to be fairly narrow as they are easier

for their small hands to hold. The length of the reins must be checked, to make sure the reins will not dangle in a long loop that could get caught around the rider's foot. (A knot could be put in the end if this was the case.) Nor should the reins be so short that they will be pulled out of the rider's hands if the horse/pony stretches its head down to the ground. Adults will find thicker reins, with some form of grip, more comfortable to hold and are less likely to let them slip through their hands.

c. For disabled riders or small children who have less control over their upper body movements, a head collar may be fitted under the horse's bridle. This is so that the reins can be attached directly to the head collar to prevent the horse's mouth from being accidentally pulled.

d. Breastplates and martingales make good neck straps as they are firmly attached to the saddle and usually sit in a position on the horse's neck that allows the rider to hold on to them without tipping forward. Neck straps that are just a loop around the horse's neck, not attached to any other part of the tack, must be long enough for the rider to hold without causing them to lean forward into a poor position. The more firmly the neck strap is attached to the tack, the more helpful it will be if the rider loses their balance sideways. A loose neck strap will slip round the horse's neck as the rider slips sideways, and therefore will not help to prevent a fall.

e. The saddle should be of a general purpose (GP) design, as a beginner rider will need to ride with fairly short stirrups to begin with. This type of saddle will accommodate the beginner more comfortably at this stage. Saddles for small ponies should have quite short saddle flaps as a small child's legs will not reach very far down the pony's sides, resulting in the child not being able to make contact with the pony when they try to use their legs.

f. It is a good idea to use one of the designs of safety iron (Peacock or Australian Simplex), to minimise the possibility of the rider's foot getting trapped. Also, make sure the irons are small enough for tiny feet and large enough for adults. When the rider's foot is in the iron – with the widest part of the rider's foot on the base of the stirrup – there should be a gap of approximately 6m–13mm on each side to prevent

Two safety irons: (far left) the Peacock Safety Iron; (left) the Australian Simplex, or bent leg iron.

the foot from becoming trapped or from swimming around in an overly large stirrup.

g. For small fat ponies a crupper is often essential to prevent the saddle from slipping forward up the ponies' neck.

h. A saddle with a rigid tree will not be as comfortable for the rider, but it will support the rider in such a way that their beginner's bumping and loss of balance will not be transmitted quite so much to the horse's back. For similar reasons as above, a fairly thick pad or numnah should be used to absorb the inevitable bumps in the saddle.

The location

a. For children on ponies, a small enclosed indoor or outdoor arena is ideal. In a small arena, approximately 20mx20m or 20mx30m, the pupil should feel quite safe, and the pony should be less inclined to pick up speed.

b. It is helpful if the arena is marked out with the usual markers, but in addition to have a picture which represents each letter. For example, an apple to represent A for apple. In this way, young children who have only just started school (four-and-a-half to five years of age) can understand more easily the instructions given by their instructor. This may also be helpful for disabled riders, depending upon the type of disability.

c. Within the arena, or close by, there should be some props available to make the lesson more interesting and demanding. Poles can be used to walk over, or to lay out a particular track to be followed. Cones are helpful as corner markers for the rider to ride around, or if laid out in a row, they can be used as a bending and steering exercise.

d. For adults a standard 20mx40m enclosed arena, indoor or outdoor, is the most suitable area to start with. The arena should be marked with the usual letters.

e. A mounting block should be available – and the instructor should teach pupils, from the start, to use it so as not to damage the horse's back and saddle, or indeed, themselves. When the rider has mastered the art of mounting from a block, he or she can occasionally practise from the ground to make sure they can cope in an emergency.

f. Similar props as those used for children's lessons will make it easier for pupil and instructor to progress.

g. For both more confident children and adults, it can be a relaxing and enjoyable end to a lesson if for the last five or ten minutes they are lead out of the enclosed school to be taken for a walk around a field or a similar area. However, it is not a good idea to go out on lanes where traffic may startle the horse or pony.

Choosing a suitable horse or pony

a. The horse or pony needs to be calm but quite forward-going for a lead rein lesson. A sluggish pony will need constant encouragement from the instructor which is likely to result in rather jerky gaits. At the same time a nervous pupil is often unnerved by the instructor needing to use the whip to encourage the pony to walk on. So a horse or pony which walks and trots out keenly is required.

b. At the same time, this horse or pony should be content to stand still without fidgeting while girths and stirrups are adjusted. It should also be of a kind temperament so the pupil can pat and talk to it before they begin the lesson.

c. As beginner riders will often make jerky, uncoordinated movements and be heavy handed with their mount, it needs to be accustomed to these actions and accept them without making any sudden reaction. For example, the rider may drag a foot over the horse's hindquarters when mounting or dismounting. Horses unaccustomed to this would be inclined to jump forward, which could lead to disastrous consequences for a beginner.

d. Horses and ponies of a quiet disposition are often quite round and perhaps a little overweight. This is not ideal for beginner riders, as they may find it difficult to stretch their legs around an overly large barrel. This is particularly true for small children on little fat ponies. It is also helpful if the horse is not too tall. A strong 15.2hh for an average adult would be far easier to cope with and less daunting for a first-time rider than a 16.2hh plus.

Length of lesson

A half-hour lesson is generally a suitable length of time for the beginner rider. Any longer is usually too tiring both physically and mentally. In fact, the rider will not even be on the horse for a full 30 minutes, as some of the time will be taken up with explanations and demonstrations on adjusting girth and stirrups, and how to mount.

How the instructor should lead the horse

a. The instructor must make sure they are always walking forward. It is a common mistake for the instructor to walk by the horse's head and then turn back to look at the pupil, ending up walking backwards. This is likely to result, for example, in the instructor bumping into a jump and possibly falling over. In this situation the instructor will be of no help to their pupil.

b. When leading on the nearside of the horse, take the lead rein in your left hand, and walk approximately level with the rider's leg. Your right hand is then free to steady a small child, or replace a poor leg position.

The instructor is positioned where she can help and steady the small child, while at the same time giving a lead rein lesson.

A stick can be carried in the left hand, and then be passed into the right hand if it is necessary to use it on the horse's hindquarters.

c. Leading in this way also prevents the instructor from taking over all control from the rider. The rider will need to be aware of guiding the horse on a straight line, to prevent it from turning towards its instructor and ending up on an ever-decreasing circle.

The content

First-time riders will need to be shown how to adjust stirrups and girths, mount up, hold reins, etc. The subjects covered in Chapter 4 should all be taught in the lead rein lesson, as the rider progresses, except perhaps with the exception of the canter. Suitable content for a lead rein lesson may include the following.

a. At the beginning of the lesson let the rider practise riding the horse in walk around the arena. Make one or two transitions to halt, and practise changing the rein. The instructor should change sides when leading so he or she is positioned towards the inside of the arena and never squashed between the horse and the fence/boards.

b. Cones can be placed in each corner to help give the rider a solid object to ride the horse around, and so he or she begins to get a feel for riding corners and not letting the horse fall in.

c. Cones can also be used in any position around the arena to help give the rider something to aim for. Small children are more likely to enjoy being asked to ride from cone to cone, rather than being asked to ride a straight turn across the school from E to B, which may be a more suitable task for an adult.

d. The rider can gradually be made familiar with simple school movements. These can include: turns up and down the centre line; changes of rein across the diagonal; and 20m circles. When he or she progresses to riding off the leading rein and joins a group lesson they will then be familiar with the directions the instructor will be giving.

e. Once the rider appears to be confident and is becoming reasonably competent at making transitions from halt to walk and walk to halt, as well as being able to guide the horse around the arena with a little help from the instructor, then it is time to venture into trot.

f. Begin with a trot down the long side of the arena, as trotting on a straight line is easier for the rider. He or she can practise using their aids to move the horse forwards into trot, then at the end of the long side returning to walk. The rider should be encouraged to ride the horse forward after the trot and try to maintain the walk, rather than collapsing into halt at the end of each trot. These transitions will prove quite demanding for a beginner rider. The instructor will need to make constant position corrections and keep reminding the rider of how to apply the aids.

g. Make sure that you give praise when it is due. If the rider shows improvement or does something well, then say so. Don't say "Good", when in fact what he or she has done is not good – this will not help them to improve. Give lots of encouragement. For example, you may say: "Well done with your rising trot that time; you kept a really good rhythm, but you've started gripping with your knees and your toes are pointing down."

h. At some point, the instructor will need to keep the horse trotting for a longer stretch, perhaps once or twice around the whole arena, in order to give the rider a chance to really establish their trot rhythm, being able to rise to the trot smoothly.

i. Take care to keep a check on how well the rider is coping with the stresses and strains of all the work. Signs of the rider becoming tired, and stressed, include: losing position; looking red in the face; losing concentration; not carrying out an exercise as well as they had previously; breathing very heavily; etc. People often don't want to admit to being tired, and children are often reluctant to speak out.

j. In order to keep the rider's interest while they keep practising these same exercises, poles and cones will help to make the lesson more interesting, especially for children. Place two or three poles at random around the school, and give the rider the task of riding the horse over the poles in walk and then eventually in trot.

k. With the use of these props, tasks can be set. For example: walk over the green and white pole, then halt at A, then walk on and trot at the cone, then turn left at the B marker, and so on. The instructor should be helping the riders, correcting them and giving them guidance throughout the task set.

l. A little work without stirrups may be used when a beginner rider is nearing the stage when he or she will be able to ride without being on a lead rein. This will help them to gain confidence in their ability to ride without stirrups so they will not be inclined to panic if they do happen to lose a stirrup accidentally.

m. Some physical exercises can be used part way through the lesson. This variation will give the instructor a rest, as he or she will have had to run around the school and be quite active during a leading rein lesson. Physical exercises, too, add to the riders' enjoyment, while improving their balance, confidence, and basic position.

n. At some point during their course of leading rein lessons, teach the riders how to carry a stick so that they can become accustomed to it and learn to change it from hand to hand.

Helpful hints on exam technique

1. Listen carefully to the examiner's brief, and ask questions if you are not absolutely sure about anything the examiner has said. You may be told that you can take the rider off the lead rein once you have assessed his or her ability, as it is often the case that the "guinea pig" riders are already riding independently in normal circumstances.

2. In an examination you will probably be teaching a rider you don't know who is riding a pony you don't know. Therefore, you should begin by introducing yourself, then find out as much as possible about the rider so you can give a suitable lesson.

3. If there is anything you are not happy about, say so straight away. For example, if the rider is not wearing safe footwear, don't assume that someone else has checked their shoes. Point the error out, as the examiner may not have noticed, and you should be demonstrating that you are capable of conducting a safe, enjoyable and educational lesson. Safe equipment for horse and rider is part of the instructor's responsibility.

4. Try to be near to the examiner if you stop to make corrections or give explanations to the rider. Otherwise the examiner will have to interrupt you and ask you to speak louder or move nearer. This can be unnerving and interrupt your train of thought and plan for the lesson.

5. As you do not know the pony and rider, do not try exercises like "round the world" for the reasons stated in Chapter 5. Err on the safe side, but make sure the lesson is not boring.

10 The Lunge Lesson

When to use this type of lesson

a. When beginner adult riders have had one or two leading rein lessons they can then progress to having a few lunge lessons. This will help them begin to establish a balanced position. If the riders were fairly confident to begin with, however, it may be that they would have been able to bypass the lead rein lessons and begin on the lunge instead.

b. Very small children should not be given lunge lessons as it is too easy for them to lose balance. Due to centrifugal force exerted on the rider when the horse is being lunged, there is a tendency for the rider to be thrown to the outside. If a fall does occur during a lunge lesson the rider will more than likely fall to the outside. This can be particularly nasty as the horse's quarters can swing out into the rider and he or she may fall against the boards or rails of the school.

c. For larger and stronger children, and for adults from beginner level upwards, lunge lessons are very helpful for improving depth of seat, balance and overall position. The lessons are also a good way of getting to grips with a particular positional fault that a rider may have developed. The instructor has control of the horse and keeps it active in walk or trot, so the rider only has to concentrate on his or her own performance.

d. Work on the lunge is particularly helpful for showing riders how their position and leg aids influence the horse, and that a great deal can be done without the use of their reins. The rider who consistently uses very strong rein aids and not enough leg, should greatly benefit from being lunged. He or she can practise making some of the transitions

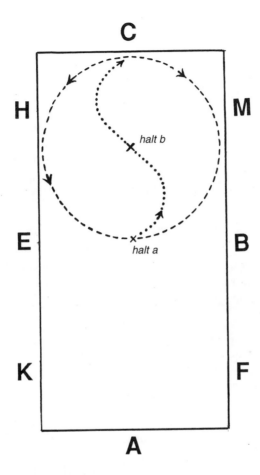

C

H   **M**

halt b

E   **B**

halt a

K   **F**

A

To change rein when lungeing halt at point a. Lead the horse across to point b and halt. Change to the other side of the horse then continue out on to the circle on the other rein.

themselves, particularly downwards from trot to walk and walk to halt, while their reins are knotted, so they only have seat and legs to use.

e. A lunge lesson offers the perfect opportunity to improve the riders' feel for what is going on underneath them. They can practise feeling for the individual footfalls at walk, and perhaps be asked to say "Now" each time one particular leg is lifted and brought forward. This could help improve their ability, for example, to ride lateral work. If they can feel when the inside hind leg is coming underneath the horse, they can use their leg aid to better effect when asking the horse to step sideways. They can also practise feeling for the trotting diagonals, so they don't need to look down to check.

f. As the instructor you need to make sure that pupils receive a mix of lunge lessons, along with their other lessons, to make sure they can put the improvement on the lunge into practice. Too many lunge lessons can begin to make a rider crooked, because of the centrifugal force throwing the rider outwards.

The instructor's equipment

a. Riding turnout should be worn.

b. Gloves are a must when lungeing, to protect your hands from rope burns if the horse pulls.

c. A hard hat should be worn, to protect your head. Although the horse should be well behaved for lungeing, horses can kick out at head height.

d. A lunge line that you feel comfortable with is important. If it is too thick or too thin, or not long enough, it will make your task very difficult. A great deal of practice is required in the art of coiling up and letting out a lunge line. There are too many commands to give and corrections to make during a lunge lesson, without the distraction of a muddled lunge line.

e. A lunge whip is needed. This should also be quite lightweight and have a good long lash. When approaching the horse, or moving around it to adjust tack, or helping the rider mount, the handle of the whip should be tucked under your arm with the main length of the whip pointing out behind you. It is not necessary to pick up the lash part of the whip during the lesson. In fact it can be dangerous to do so as the horse may misinterpret your action as a move to use the whip on it.

The horse's or pony's equipment

a. For beginner riders a GP saddle is best, as their position will not yet be sufficiently developed to accommodate the straight-cut dressage saddle. As riders progress, a dressage saddle will help them to sit well.
b. The horse's normal snaffle bridle should be used, with the noseband removed to allow for a comfortable fit with the lunge cavesson that is required.
c. A neck strap is useful for all levels of rider.
d. The horse should wear boots on all four legs to protect against knocks,

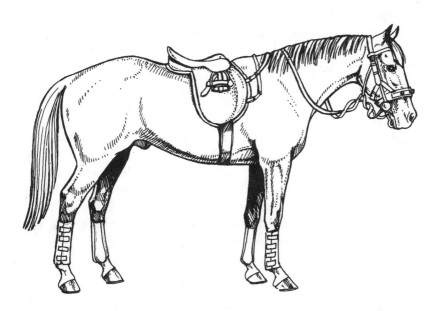

A horse equipped for a lunge lesson and ready to work.

which are more likely when working continuously on a circle especially if the rider occasionally unbalances the horse.

e. Side reins will be needed to provide a contact for the instructor to work the horse into. This helps to keep the horse's gaits smooth and balanced for the rider. Side reins are also necessary for maintaining control which is essential when you have a rider on the horse.

The location

An enclosed arena, either indoors or outside, is the safest area for lungeing horse and rider. Although horses can be lunged in a field without a rider, the effect that open space has on most horses could lead to a dangerous situation once a rider is mounted.

Choosing a suitable horse or pony

a. For the instructor, it is a difficult task teaching the rider, handling the equipment, and keeping control of the horse. Therefore, the lunge horse needs to work easily in a good outline and be calm and obedient, but fairly forward-going if you are going to be able to carry out the lesson effectively.

b. Beginner riders need a horse with gaits that are not too extravagant, that will "tick over" in a regular trot rhythm while they learn to find balance both sitting and rising.

c. More advanced riders need a horse schooled to a more advanced level so they can learn to balance and move with changes of gait within the gaits and feel the quality of gait they should be looking for.

d. Not many horses have a balanced enough canter for lunge work. If the horse is able to canter in a steady manner on a 20m circle while maintaining its balance, rhythm and outline, then it will be a very useful horse for giving lunge lessons.

Length of lesson

a. Lunge work is a strenuous activity for the horse. It is required to work constantly on a circle and quite often mainly in trot. The work is even harder for the horse when it is being ridden as well. For this reason, a half-hour session is the most suitable length of time.

b. The rider will also feel quite tired after the half-hour, as this is a very intensive one-to-one lesson.

c. It may be necessary to book a lesson which will occupy a session of 45 minutes or one hour, as some aspects of the lunge lesson take up extra time. For example, the horse needs to be worked in before the rider is mounted. The adjustment of side reins at the beginning and possibly during the lesson also takes time. If only a half-hour period has been booked, the rider may end up receiving only 15 minutes of instruction.

The content

a. Following the usual lesson structure, you should introduce yourself and find out if the rider has been lunged before. It is necessary to explain that when being lunged the instructor is in control of the horse and the rider should only use leg or rein aids if told to do so. The main purpose of the lesson is to let the rider concentrate on their position and not have to worry about the horse.

b. You should then work the horse in before the rider is mounted. Make sure the reins and stirrups are secured in the usual way for lungeing. You now have an opportunity to warm the horse up, making sure it is listening to your voice and going forward in a manner that will give the rider smooth gaits to work with.

c. Whilst working the horse you should keep the rider involved. Having asked him or her to stand to one side, safely out of the way, you can point out to them how the horse is working, for example when it is tracking up.

d. When the horse has been sufficiently worked in, the rider can mount up. Rider and instructor together can prepare the horse by adjusting stirrups, tightening the girth, and removing the reins from the throat latch.

e. Side reins must be undone when the horse is at rest and the rider is mounting. The side reins will have been adjusted for trot work and therefore will restrict the horse if left attached when at halt, and may cause the horse to resist and panic if it moves and feels the restriction when being mounted. Always undo the side reins when adjusting tack, mounting or dismounting.

f. Once the rider is on the horse and ready to begin, the side reins can be re-attached. You must make sure you walk the horse forward and out on to the circle. Don't try to turn it immediately to the side, as the side reins will stop it from being able to turn. Therefore, it is important to have halted the horse in a good position to begin with. The middle of the circle is usually the best place to stop and start from.

g. To begin with ask the rider to adopt their usual position in the saddle. He or she should be told to take up the reins but not to take a contact, as the side reins are providing the contact for the horse. If the horse feels two slightly opposing contacts, it can make it hollow and resist, and in some cases panic.

The lesson

a. The first few minutes are a time for the rider to work in and get a feel of the horse's gaits, a time for the horse to adjust to the rider, and a time for the instructor to look at and assess the rider's good and bad points. You should see the rider in walk, and trot, both sitting and rising.

b. Remember that you need to prepare both horse and rider for all the transitions. Tell the rider what you intend to do, then use the horse's name so it now knows that you are talking to it, and then give the usual commands. As the horse will respond to words like "Trot" and "Walk", when you are speaking to the rider use the phrases "Upwards and downwards transitions" – this avoids the horse coming forward to walk, for example, the moment you tell the rider to prepare for walk. So you may say to the rider, "Prepare for a downwards transition", then say the horse's name and "Walk".

c. Having assessed the rider, bring the horse forward to halt, ready to change the rein. While you are at the horse's head is a good time to have the rider quit and cross their stirrups, check the girth, and make adjustments to side reins if necessary. Remember to lead the horse forward into the middle of the circle, so you can change the rein smoothly.

d. While working the rider without stirrups, you can also relieve him or her of the need to hold the reins. A knot should be tied in the reins, but the rider should keep one finger through the buckle end to prevent them from slipping down the horse's neck where they could become dangerous.

e. It is a good idea to have the rider rest their outside hand, with a finger through the reins, on the pommel. He or she can then grasp the pommel for security if they begin to lose balance. At the same time, having the outside hand on the pommel gently brings the rider's outside shoulder forward into a good position to follow the line of the circle.

f. You can now work on correcting any problems you have noticed in the rider. You may use one or two physical exercises, but only if they are appropriate for that rider. Use transitions from halt to walk and walk to trot and down again to test the rider's ability to maintain balance and a good position through all the changes of gait.

g. It is quite common that riders, for example, allow their legs to slip forward and their heels to come up as their horse makes a transition from walk to trot. This is because they are tensing during the transition and not yet deep enough in their seat to maintain balance. If this happens, tell the rider what you can see him or her doing, then repeat the exercise helping them to overcome the problem. You may say, "Relax your seat, and carry your upper body, while stretching your legs down. Try to let your seat and hips move softly with the horse as it makes the transition. Breathe slowly and concentrate on remaining relaxed."

h. If the rider is looking quite neat and balanced, you may work on feel for footfalls and diagonals.

i. During the lesson you need to change the rein, perhaps twice more. Don't change rein so frequently that the rider never has time to settle into his or her work, but make sure you see them from both sides, as most riders look much better on one rein than the other.

j. Towards the end of the lesson the rider should take back the stirrups and reins so you can assess the rider again, and see if he or she has improved the original problems you noted. Tell them what you see and ask them if they can feel any improvement.

k. Try to finish on a good note. Make sure the rider remains mounted until you have unclipped the side reins.

Points to note

1. It is vital that the instructor works the horse in such a way that the rider has smooth transitions and gaits to work with. The rider cannot hope to improve balance and position if the horse is being idle and making jerky transitions.

2. Always tell riders what problems you see, it will then make more sense to them when you make a correction. You should always try to make the corrections positive, by saying how to correct the problem, not just pointing out what they are doing wrong. For example:

   — The instructor sees that the rider is tipping forward.
   — The instructor says, "Jane, you are tending to tip forward so your shoulders are in front of the vertical. This is putting you out of balance."
   — The instructor makes a positive correction, saying, "Bring your upper body a little further back so your shoulders are in a vertical line above your hips."

Common rider faults and problems

1. Many riders tip forward or get left behind and tip backwards with their upper body during transitions. You need to look for this and tell the riders what you see. Ask if they can feel this happening, and then have them practise transitions working on improving this point. Make sure you look for the cause of the problem. Are they tipping because they are anticipating and tensing during the transition? Or, is it because their legs are badly positioned so they cannot keep their balance? Or, is it because their seat is not central and relaxed in the saddle? Always

(Opposite page) *The rider must work to achieve the correct balanced position. Here* (top) *she is out of balance, with her legs pushed forward and her seat at the back of the saddle; her seat* (centre) *is now in the deepest part of the saddle but her upper body is collapsed and her heels drawing up; now* (below) *she is in a good balanced position.*

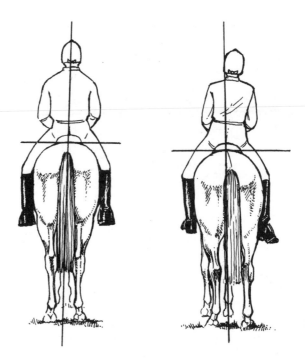

A rider working to achieve the correct balanced position. Here (left) *he is in a good central position; but* (right) *is incorrectly collapsing his inside hip – an error instructors should be alert to at all times.*

look for the root of the problem, which is more often than not in the seat, otherwise you will never correct it.

2. When being lunged, it is easy for riders to collapse their inside hip and lean in with their seat slipping to the outside. This can be difficult for a less experienced instructor to see. Tell the riders to check their position and put a little more weight on their inside seat bone. Explain to them why this is necessary on the lunge. Make them aware of the problem so you can keep reminding them by saying, "Make sure you are not

leaning in." When you change the rein, take the opportunity to stop and check that they are sitting centrally.
3. As already mentioned, some riders' legs will often slip forward and grip upwards, with heels drawing up and toes sticking out. The root of this problem is nearly always the seat. Riders must be central and relaxed before they can hope to keep their legs in a good position. Help the riders to find a good balanced position in the saddle and then, as they practise transitions keeping that position, constantly correct them. Hopefully, they will make progress.

Helpful hints on exam technique
1. You should not begin the lesson with any preconceived ideas about the rider's ability. Assess the person in front of you and teach accordingly. Make sure your work is progressive by starting the rider gently with reins and stirrups and then progress to taking stirrups and reins away if you think the rider capable.
2. Many candidates make the mistake of working through a series of exercises whether they are relevant to the rider or not. You must have enough experience to be able to see the main rider problems and use exercises that are relevant to them.
3. Try not to fall into the trap of doings things differently for the exam. Candidates often say they didn't like to use the lunge whip on the horse in case it wasn't allowed in an exam, or that they didn't like to walk a circle for the same reason, and so on. If the horse is being idle and needs a tap with the whip, then do it, that is what the whip is for. In the same way, if you need to walk a circle within the lunge circle in order to be more effective with the whip, then do so. The sort of things you shouldn't do are those which could be unsafe, or detrimental to the rider and horse. So, don't crack the whip; it may cause any other horses in the school to shoot off. Don't use exercises not relevant to the rider. Don't turn the horse in a tight circle with the side reins restricting it. Don't let the lunge line dangle on the ground where the horse could get its legs caught up, etc.
4. Your lungeing technique is also being examined. You cannot be responsible for giving a rider a safe, informative and effective lunge lesson if

your lungeing is ineffective and/or not safe. You must have enough lungeing practice to be safe and effective in your handling of the equipment.

5. Although you only have a short time to show your skills, try not to hurry to the extent that you spoil the lesson. Keep the horse's warm-up time to an absolute minimum. It will probably have been warmed-up already. If there is a problem with the equipment, tell your examiner so it can be rectified quickly. Don't worry if you only manage to change the rein once during the lesson. As long as you have seen the rider on both reins, it is far more important that you demonstrate good quality teaching skills.

6. At PTT level there is no harm in using canter when warming-up the horse, provided that you are confident in your lungeing abilities. However, once the rider is mounted, canter should not be used in case both horse and rider are not capable of maintaining balance on the circle.

11 The Private Lesson

When to use this type of lesson

a. A private lesson can benefit all levels of rider. It provides an opportunity for one-to-one instruction, and is likely to produce greater rider improvement within a set time.
b. Riders who have just progressed from leading rein lessons may want to continue with private lessons to help bring them up to a standard that will allow them to join in a group lesson at a particular level.
c. Some riders may like to have a mix of private lessons along with their other riding sessions. For example, they may have a private lesson once a month to help clarify and improve areas of their riding that need particular attention.
d. Private lessons can be particularly helpful to those riders with their own horses. They may need help with improving their horse or pony as well as themselves.
e. More advanced riders usually favour private lessons and are generally better able to cope with what are more intensive sessions.

The instructor's equipment

a. Instructors will need full riding turnout of a suitable nature for the lesson. It is quite likely that they will find the need to ride the horse at some point during the lesson. This may be to school the horse, or to demonstrate a point to the rider.
b. If it is to be a dressage lesson, they will need their schooling whip; if a

jumping lesson a jumping whip. They may like to use a body protector for jumping.

c. If the lesson is to be in a field, cones or dressage markers will be useful.

d. For a jumping lesson the instructor may need an assistant to help with moving jumps.

The horse's or pony's equipment

The horse simply needs to be wearing its usual tack suitable for the type of lesson. If the owner has different equipment for different disciplines, then the type of lesson should be agreed so a dressage or jumping saddle, boots, etc., can be worn as appropriate.

The location

a. An indoor or outdoor arena generally offers a good surface and safe area for this type of lesson. However, there are other options.

b. A field could be used if a horse and rider are preparing for a jumping competition on grass.

c. If preparing for dressage competitions, where the arenas will be marked out on grass, then laying out an arena in a field will help to accustom horse and rider to this type of surface and riding within dressage boards.

d. If it is to be a cross-country lesson, then suitable woodland or fields will need to be available.

e. If there is any doubt about the horse's behaviour or the rider's ability to maintain control, then a safely enclosed area is a must.

Choosing a suitable horse or pony

a. If the rider has his or her own horse or pony, then there are no choices and the instructor will need to try and work the two together whether they are well matched or not.

b. If the lesson is taking place using riding school horses, make sure you know enough about the rider's ability and what they hope to gain from the lesson. You can then choose a confidence-giving jumping horse, or dressage schoolmaster, etc.

c. Be careful not to "over horse" beginner pupils. They may well seem confident and quite capable on the lunge or lead rein, but will quickly lose confidence if their horse or pony takes charge and runs off with them.

Length of lesson

a. At beginner level a half-hour lesson is usually a good length of time. The rider will be using muscles not usually used, and trying to take in terms he or she is unfamiliar with, as well as concentrating on learning to master new riding skills. They are likely to deteriorate and lose concentration if a longer session is used, although this is not always the case.

b. For more advanced riders, particularly those that are fitter due to riding regularly, an hour is a good length of time. Quite a lot of work can be covered during this time. The horse should also be able to work for an hour if it is fit for the job. After this period of time the horse will probably need a break to stop the work becoming too physically and mentally tiring.

The content

This will obviously depend on horse and rider and their aims.

a. For beginner lessons try to give the rider plenty of opportunity to practise maintaining walk, trot, and canter around the arena and when riding circles and turns.

b. Much of the work will be very repetitive at this stage, as a beginner needs frequent and continual practice if he or she is to improve both coordination and balance. Keep the lessons simple, and add interest by teaching school figures. Make sure you are continuously pointing out to the rider where improvement can be made, followed by instructions as to how to make that improvement.

c. Beginner children having private lessons need plenty of fun to keep their interest. This usually means lots of trotting and cantering, so be careful to give the pony plenty of breathers. At the same time you must make sure you insist on the rider giving the correct aids and keep a check on the rider's position.

d. Work for high standards from the start, then the rider will not have to overcome bad habits at a later stage. Avoid complicated technical explanations for children, just keep everything simple but correct. Ask questions frequently to check understanding.

e. More advanced riders, adults particularly, usually appreciate having the aids for various movements explained more fully. Every effort should be made to check and improve the riders' understanding.

f. For riders who have progressed beyond the beginner level, more work on school figures, transitions, pole work, etc., can be included. How much will depend on a rider's specific needs.

g. Follow the usual lesson structure. Spend the first few minutes of the lesson warming-up and assessing the horse and rider, then go on to include practice in one or more of the subjects from Chapters 4 to 8.

h. Always give plenty of praise and encouragement to riders, but do not fall into the trap of telling them they have done well when they haven't really shown any improvement. Don't tell them what they have done is good if it isn't. Tell them if it was a little better, or better in some aspects, if it was, and go on to tell them what was not so good.

i. Remember that private lessons are very intensive as you are working on a one-to-one basis. Give your rider frequent rest periods. Look for signs of fatigue. Avoid long periods of sitting trot, or working without stirrups and canter. Especially if the rider only rides once a week.

Helpful hints on exam technique

1. A private lesson is not given in the PTT exam. However, the pros and cons of private lessons (as outlined at the start of this chapter) will be discussed in the theory section of the exam.

2. From a riding school's business point of view, private lessons do not earn the school as much money per hour as a group lesson. Therefore, instructors should try to make sure that there are plenty of pupils riding in groups, and not to encourage too many private bookings.

12 The Group Lesson

When to use this type of lesson

a. When several people of the same riding standard are all able to ride at the same time, it is the ideal time to form a group.

b. Group lessons are ideal for riding school instruction, as they earn more money per hour for one instructor, and are likely to be the main source of income for the business.

c. From the rider's point of view, and for subsidised Pony Club or riding club teaching, the group lesson is a less expensive way for each rider to receive instruction.

d. For children, in particular, group instruction can be more fun. It also adds a more competitive element to each lesson for those individuals who enjoy that type of incentive.

e. For some adult riders a group lesson once a week is very much a social occasion, as well as an opportunity to improve their riding skills.

f. For those riders who only ride once a week, group lessons provide the opportunity to ride for an hour, but with less intensive instruction which may otherwise be too tiring.

The instructor's equipment

a. Neat and practical riding turnout is required so the instructor can ride and demonstrate if necessary wearing suitable clothing for the weather and location. Don't forget to wear a watch.

b. Props may be needed; for example, if teaching at a Pony Club rally in a field. You may not be supplied with markers, so it will be very helpful to your teaching if you have some cones or markers to make an arena with.

c. A suitable horse may be needed if you intend to take your group for cross-country instruction.

d. When teaching a group of small children it is advisable to have at least one assistant. The children will need help with girths, stirrups, getting on, etc. If you do not have an assistant, it will take most of the lesson time just to organise the children.

e. You may also need assistants to lead riders if you have a beginner group whose members are not yet capable of keeping control on their own.

The horse's or pony's equipment

a. Riders with their own horses should be informed, before the lesson, about the intended subject matter. They can then select appropriate equipment for that type of lesson. They may have a dressage saddle, a particular bridle for jumping, or protective boots for cross-country riding, etc., that they would like to use.

b. Riding school horses should be tacked up for the riders, with the correct equipment.

c. As the instructor, it is your responsibility to check the tack of all the horses before commencement of the lesson. Make sure girths are firm, that all tack fits comfortably, and that it is in serviceable condition. Any tack not suitable or safe must be replaced before the start of the lesson.

The location

a. Group lessons for beginners and small children should take place in an enclosed area. An indoor or outdoor school with an all-weather surface is ideal. However, a small paddock can be used if it is relatively flat and the ground is not muddy or very hard and slippery.

b. For Pony Club or riding club rallies you may take the lesson in part of a field. Using a corner of the field so you have two enclosed sides is helpful. If you are teaching a group of small children or very novice riders, it is also preferable not to use an area too far from the gate or horsebox area. If any of the ponies are "nappy" and try to return to the boxes against their riders' wishes, they will not have too far to go and will therefore be less likely to gather speed and get over-excited.

c. When giving cross-country lessons you will inevitably be in more open spaces. Where possible, try to use fields where you can be prepared for loose horses. Close any gates that will help you retain control in a fairly enclosed area.

Choosing a suitable horse or pony

a. When providing horses for riders, try to give each rider a fair selection. For example, make sure that a small adult does not always end up riding a pony unless the rider makes a particular request to do so.

b. If a group of riders have progressed to a fairly competent level when working in the school on the flat, take care not to over-horse them for riding outside cross-country. It would be better to under-horse them a little, until you have found out how competent and confident they are when riding in open spaces and jumping.

c. When riders are mounted on their own horses you need to assess the individual animals. Proceed with caution until you have found out some of their good and bad points. Not many riders like to be left out of a particular exercise because you feel that they or their horses cannot manage it. Try to use exercises suitable for all the horses and riders in the group.

d. For these riders with their own horses, it may be necessary to give advice about future training to help a particular rider overcome certain problems with their horse.

e. Occasionally a horse or pony is found to have characteristics that make it dangerous to use in a group lesson. For example, it may be particularly inclined to go out of its way to kick other horses, or it may run at others with teeth bared, or may even try to savage another horse. These horses and ponies should only be used for private lessons as such vices only create a problem when the horse is ridden in company.

Length of lesson

a. A one-hour session is most suitable for group lessons with once a week riders or children. This allows sufficient time to make improvement without exhausting horses and riders.
b. Group sessions for riders with their own horses may benefit from being a little longer, perhaps 90 minutes. If riders have transported their horses to a school for the lesson, a slightly longer session will make their journey more worthwhile. Providing horse and rider are fit enough, this length of lesson will allow more time for a combination of flat work and jumping to be taught.
c. The number of riders in the group lesson will also make a difference to how long you spend. If there are only four or five riders, then each will receive plenty of attention within a one-hour session. If you have a larger group of up to ten riders, then a longer session will enable you to give each rider more attention. A group of six to eight is a more manageable size. More than that makes it an exhausting session for the instructor, and will cause some frustration for the riders as they have to wait for their turn to carry out an exercise.

The content

The following are a selection of exercises that work well with groups of riders. Some work better with novice groups and some with more experienced groups. Within this format of exercises you should be progressively teaching all the subject matter outlined in Chapters 4 to 8.

a. With a group of riders you are not familiar with, begin the ride in closed order. If you know the horses, choose an order that you know is appropriate, with longer striding horses in front, and any horse that kicks at the back. If you don't know the horses, ask if any of them kick, then choose the largest to be lead file, working back to the smallest and those likely to kick.

b. With the ride keeping one horse's distance between each of them, see each lead file go forward to working trot, rising, and trot to the rear of the ride. Make sure each rider prepares the downwards transition to walk well before they reach the rear of the ride so they do not get too close to the horse in front. If the riders appear to be quite competent, you can send the next rider into trot before the first rider has reached the rear of the ride.

c. Send the whole ride forward to trot as a ride, and change the rein across the diagonal, then return to walk. You will now have seen each rider trot and make transitions to and from walk, so you should have a good idea of their weak and strong points by now.

d. Next, see each rider go forward to sitting trot in preparation for canter, pick up canter in the first available corner, and canter to the rear of the ride. If you would like to see them maintain canter for a longer stretch, then they should be told to include a 20m circle at the free end of the school before going to join the rear of the ride. Again, stress the need to prepare the downwards transitions in good time so they do not get too close to the horse in front.

e. Having seen each rider in canter, you should be able to decide if they are capable of riding in open order. First check they understand what is meant by open order, and explain if necessary, then move them out into open order. To do this, you could tell the rear file to halt at a certain marker, while the rest of the ride keep in walk. Then tell the next rear file where to halt and so on, until each of the riders has halted equally spaced out around the school. Alternatively, you could have each lead file trot on into a space, or all the riders circle away from each other into a space. Once they are spaced out evenly, tell them to keep well spaced and circle away if they find themselves starting to catch up with the rider in front.

f. Once in open order, continue to work the group as a ride, and see them ride 20m circles, serpentines, turns up and down the centre line, across the school, or across the diagonals, either in trot or walk. Not forgetting that you can also see the riders go forward to halt. You should be checking their ability to ride accurate movements, smooth transitions, including square halts, to keep a good position, apply the aids correctly, and ride their horses forward between leg and hand, showing an ability to think ahead and consider the other riders. They will need constant help from you, so you should be correcting them and telling them how to improve. Always make sure you follow corrections through. There is no point in saying "Bring your lower leg further back", if the rider then fails to make the correction. You must go on telling them to move their lower leg, until they have achieved an improved position. Remember, ground poles can be used to make the exercises more interesting and demanding.

g. Now is also a good time to see some work without stirrups. They have had a chance to work in, and you will have seen the riders walk, trot and canter. You will now know if the riders are capable of working safely without stirrups, but just check with them that they are happy to do so. The length of time you spend without stirrups will depend on rider fitness. Don't overdo it. More experienced riders can be asked to canter without stirrups as well, but make sure you have seen them canter with their stirrups first, so you are sure they are going to be safe.

h. With a small group of experienced riders, it is possible to have the whole ride canter together in open order. You must feel that they are capable of circling away and keeping their distance while in canter. If you have any doubts about their ability or how their horses will behave, then put the ride back in closed order and see the riders canter individually again.

i. Another exercise to use for individual canters, one that is a little more testing than the front to rear canter, is as follows. Rear files in turn, take an inner track and go forward to trot. Trot past the ride and on reaching the front, make a transition to canter. Canter to the rear of the ride, go forward to trot, and trot to the front of the ride. Go forward to walk and take up the position of lead file.

j. For more experienced riders, you could see them ride a figure-of-eight in canter, showing changes of canter lead through trot. For this exercise you would need to have the ride halted while one rider at a time rides the exercise. This can be a good exercise for small groups, but for larger groups it will entail too much standing around for the riders waiting to take their turn.

k. Another canter exercise, frequently used, involves the main part of the group riding a 15m circle in one end of the school, while one rider leaves the group, rides forward to canter, and goes large. They then ride a 20m circle in the free end of the school, then return to trot and rejoin the circle with the other riders. In my opinion, this exercise is only useful for much more experienced riders and should not be used for novices. The riders left on the 15m circle tend to wander aimlessly around an irregular shape, causing their horses to switch off to the leg aids and become resistant. The instructor's attention is focused on the individual riding the canter and the lesson deteriorates into one of private instruction, rather than the group instruction it should be. It would be far more beneficial to have the riders in halt, so they can rest, and watch, and learn from the other rider and by listening to the instructor's comments.

l. It is generally best to keep canter exercises simple, as the canter itself and canter transitions are usually demanding enough for the rider, without adding in complicated ground plans.

m. Jumping exercises and pole work can also be introduced as the lesson progresses, if the riders are experienced enough. Always try to link the flat work and jumping together, otherwise riders forget the instruction you have been giving, with regard to turns and circles, etc. They will only realise how important it is if you explain that the horse cannot perform well over fences if the track and gait between the fences is not up to scratch.

Points to note

1. When teaching group lessons always try to keep the whole group involved. Avoid any exercises that leave out part of the ride for extended periods, as mentioned in "k." above. If part of the group are standing still, keep them involved by giving them points to look for in

the work of the rider who is carrying out the exercise.

2. Make sure when teaching a group that you really do teach, and not just direct them through a series of exercises. Having explained the exercise, and started the riders off, make sure you then help and correct them.

3. When you move on to instruction over poles, using them as discussed in Chapter 8, make sure the riders never follow one behind the other in closed order. Each horse and rider must be able to see the poles clearly, and need time to circle away from the poles if they are knocked out of line by the horse in front. Also, the horse in front may rush or jump the poles, and riders behind will need to circle away and make sure their horse does not follow suit. Keep the riders in open order and stress that they should only approach the poles if the horse before them is well clear of them.

4. If progressing to jumping, then it is sometimes necessary to have the ride in halt, while each rider approaches individually. As long as the riders are kept alert, so they ride forward to take their turn as soon as the other rider is returning to walk, then everyone can be kept moving, and standing still time is kept to a minimum. If the riders are capable, and the school area is large enough, try to keep everyone on the move, and call out each rider individually when you would like them to approach the jumps. Be careful to make sure that the rider jumping will not be riding into the other riders when landing. Good ride control is essential at all times.

5. If you are going on to work over a small course of fences, then riders should stand in the corners of the school with their horses' quarters to the wall.

6. You should stand where you can see your whole group all of the time. If you stand in the middle of the school and walk in a circle, you will inevitably have your back to some of the riders some of the time. You will not be able to see accidents about to happen. It is also more difficult for some riders to hear you some of the time. Stand near to a corner, where you can see the whole school. The riders will only be out of your sight as they pass behind you momentarily. Obviously, there will be times when you need to move. For example, for pole work and

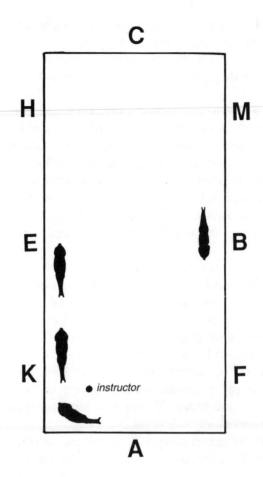

Where the instructor should stand when teaching, to be able to see the whole school and whole ride.

jumping you will need to be near the poles to replace them if and when they are knocked out of line.

Common rider faults and problems

1. As riders often tend to look down when riding in a group, they may find themselves riding too close to the other riders, getting in the way of other riders, or actually colliding with them. You must make sure you frequently tell the riders to look up, plan ahead, and make way for each other. For this reason, riding as part of a group is an excellent way of improving a rider's reactions and coordination.

2. Group riding also helps to improve self-discipline in each rider. As the instructor's time is divided between the riders, when they are not being given a specific correction, they need to be riding independently and correcting themselves. Many riders are lazy about this; immediately the instructor stops speaking to them they allow bad habits to return. Try to encourage riders to correct themselves.

Helpful hints on exam technique

1. Make sure you understand your lesson subject. If there is anything you are not absolutely clear about, ask your examiner.

2. At the beginning of the lesson, introduce yourself to your group, check their tack and find out their names. Do try to remember names, it will make your job easier, and create a better rapport with the riders. Go on to explain what you intend to do in the lesson. Then make sure you explain each exercise, and the purpose of the exercise, as you progress through the lesson. Candidates often tell riders to do something, but do not explain why. There must be a purpose to everything you do.

3. If you are working the ride in closed order and find that the order of horses you have chosen is not working, do not be afraid to change the horse order around. Likewise, do change from closed to open order and back again as many times as you like, as long as the riders know what is expected of them, and you insist on the distances set being kept. For example, you may have the ride in open order while working over trotting poles, then put them in closed order when you move on

to do a canter exercise. You may then return to the trotting pole work, and put them in open order again.

4. Probably the most common reason for candidates not reaching the required standard, is that they do not actually teach the ride. For example, the candidate may give an exercise to be ridden, and tell the riders they must not cut the corners, and should use their inside leg, etc. However, when the group ride the exercise, they *do* cut the corners and *don't* apply the correct aids, and the candidate does not correct them or follow through the corrections to a point of improvement. This candidate is just giving directions, not teaching.

5. Do pay attention to safety, but don't make the lesson boring. It is possible to be safe and not boring, and essential if the riders are going to learn and enjoy themselves. If riders are bored, they will "switch off" and certainly think twice about paying to have another lesson with that particular instructor. You don't need to use complicated exercises to make a lesson interesting, you just need to be involved, be enthusiastic, and teach.

6. Make sure you speak clearly and don't whisper or gabble. Stand where your examiner can hear you and try to project your voice so your riders can hear you easily as well. Long silences do not give your riders confidence, but a continuous, rapid, barrage of corrections are difficult to take in. Try to strike a happy medium.

7. You may teach the lesson in one half of a large school, while another candidate teaches in the other half. It is not a good idea to use jumping exercises that necessitate your riders jumping directly towards the other ride, until you are sure your riders are safe and under control, in case they lose control and end up in the other end of the school. Begin by jumping away from the other ride, then, all being well, the jump could be ridden in the other direction. If you have any doubts or problems, then explain your predicament to your examiner, and he or she will help you with the problem.

8. Candidates often fall into the trap of running out of time and not being able to fulfil their lesson brief. If the examiner feels that you have given a good lesson so far, and taught well, this will not necessarily affect the result. However, if the candidate is avoiding the pole work or jumping

part of the lesson, due to lack of confidence and knowledge, then it is likely to effect the result. You have about 35 minutes of teaching time, which is not long when you have to include pole work or jumping. For example, the lesson subject may be worded as having two parts. Assess and work towards improving the pupils' ability to make turns and half circles to enable them to make better approaches to two or three fences in the second part of your lesson. This is so the examiner can assess your ability to teach both work on the flat and with poles and/or jumping. You do not have to divide your lesson exactly in two. As soon as you have seen the riders walk, trot, and canter, using various school movements, so you can help them with their turns and circles, you can ask them to shorten their stirrups in preparation for jumping. Continue with helping to improve their turns and circles, but also now include poles in preparation for jumping, and help them to prepare for jumping, and achieving a good position over the fence.

13 Instructional Hacks and Hacking in General

When to use this type of lesson

a. Any rider who has instruction on a regular basis should benefit from the enjoyable aspects of riding out on a hack. It is a chance for the rider to put into practice all he or she has been learning in lessons, but in a more relaxed way. Through being more relaxed, the rider is often able to ride more effectively.

b. When beginner riders have progressed to a reasonable level of competence, riding out in the countryside can give them a great sense of achievement, and inspire them to go on working at improving their riding skills.

c. As the horse is moving over undulating terrain, and being faced with external influences such as birds suddenly flying up from bushes, or a plastic bag flapping on the verge, the rider becomes accustomed to dealing with the unexpected. As a result, riders who have learnt most of their riding skills in enclosed school areas, will now learn more about balance and coordination when riding out. It should also speed up their reactions.

d. Young children can be taken out on a hack on the lead rein, if they are too small to control a pony on their own. This gives them a chance to go further than the confines of a school, adding greater enjoyment to their riding and will encourage them to go on learning.

e. All riders should find horses more forward-going and keen when out hacking. This gives them a greater sense of how the horse should feel when it is working happily, as well as illustrate to them how important it is to be able to ride well in order to remain in control.

The instructor's equipment

a. You must be mounted on a suitable horse. If you are taking a group of novices, it is not helpful to ride a nervous youngster. Your horse should give a sensible lead to the rest of the ride, remain calm in an emergency, be well mannered to lead from, and be suitable for one of the riders to ride home on if something should happen to their mount.

b. It is a good idea to carry a lead rein, which can be clipped to one of the "D" rings on the saddle. You should also have a note of the telephone number of the riding centre, and some means of making a telephone call. This may be change for a telephone box, a telephone card, or a mobile telephone. A hoof pick can be helpful. These items can be carried quite comfortably in a "bum" bag around your waist.

c. You should always have a second escort to help you with the ride. This rider could bring up the rear of the ride and make sure everyone keeps together, or you could bring up the rear while your assistant leads the way. If you are giving instruction to the riders, you may like to move along the ride, talking to each rider as you go. Your assistant should also ride a sensible horse and carry a lead rein.

d. Apart from the usual riding turnout, you should equip yourself and your assistant with fluorescent and reflective clothing in the form of tabards, hat covers, etc.

The horse's or pony's equipment

a. For riding out, each horse should be in a GP saddle. Some of the horses may be ridden in a stronger bit for hacking, but this should only be the case if the horse is being ridden by an experienced rider.

b. All the equipment, as for any riding, must be completely safe and secure, and not likely to break under the strain of cantering across country.

c. It is a good idea to equip at least some of the horses with fluorescent and reflective clothing. This could be in the form of exercise sheets or leg bands, etc.

d. It is vital that horses going on a hack are well shod. Shoes that have become worn will be very slippery on the roads, and therefore not safe. A loose and then lost shoe on a hack is a big problem as the horse may be lame, or become lame. You cannot just put the horse back into its stable, as you would if it lost a shoe during a lesson. You still have to get the horse home.

e. In some areas, permits are required for riding in certain areas. If this is the case, make sure all the horses are equipped with the permit discs as necessary.

f. Ponies ridden by small children can be kept under control more easily if fitted with "grass reins". These are two pieces of cord attached to the "D" rings on the saddle, taken along and through the loop of the browband on each side of the bridle, then down to clip on to the bit rings. This allows the pony freedom to move normally, but if it tries to put its head down to eat grass, a movement that often pulls a small rider out of the saddle, it is restricted from doing so.

g. No matter how experienced the rider, it is helpful to equip each horse with a neck strap. This can be a simple strap around the horse's neck, or a martingale or breastplate neck strap.

Choosing a suitable horse or pony

a. Some horses and ponies that are good for riding lessons in the school, may not be suitable for taking on hacks. They may be too excitable, inclined to buck, be traffic shy, or have a tendency to set off very fast during canters. Whatever the problem, they are best left at home, or ridden out occasionally by experienced members of staff to give them a change of scene.

b. Conversely, some horses and ponies not suitable for school lessons may be very good out on hacks. They may be slow and stubborn in the school, or rather stiff and one-sided, but be quiet and safe for riding out in the countryside.

c. It is generally better to slightly "under-horse" riders to begin with, until you know how they are going to cope with hacking, and until they have had time to adjust to how differently some horses behave when out of the school environment.

d. The horses and ponies chosen need to work happily in a single file string. They should not be inclined to kick, buck, or become particularly excitable, and they need to be patent safety in traffic.

Length of hack

a. This will often depend on the area available for hacking. In some places it may be possible to take novices and children on an enjoyable half-hour round trip. However, in many places it may take 15 minutes or so to reach an area where the riders can have a trot or canter, so a half-hour session would not be long enough.

b. For most riding schools, a one-hour hack is long enough to reach areas where the riders can trot and canter, it is a good length of time for the horses to be working, and any longer would be too tiring for the riders.

c. For riders who ride more frequently, and are therefore more riding fit, it may be possible to stay out for up to two hours, providing you are in an area that offers plenty of countryside to ride around. You must be sure the horses are fit enough as well. Trekking centres will take riders out all day, but this is a different type of riding centre, catering for different requirements.

Preparation for the hack

a. As the instructor responsible for the hack you should check that a suitable selection of horses is provided for the riders. Check tack and shoes as mentioned.

b. Make sure you have your own equipment, horse, and escort rider prepared to go.

c. Check that all of the riders are correctly dressed for hacking out. They must have safe footwear and riding hats of the most up-to-date BSI standard. Also look at their other clothing. Coats should not be loose and flapping, they need to be done up. If they have hoods on their coats, it is a good idea to ensure that they are tucked in so they cannot become caught up on branches. In fine weather, all riders must wear long sleeves to protect their arms. Encourage all riders to wear gloves, they will be much more comfortable.

d. Once each rider is mounted, make sure they have checked their girths and adjusted their stirrups to a suitable length. Look to see that no rider has stirrup irons that are too large or too small.

e. When the whole group is ready to depart, you must establish some ground rules before you set off. Explain to the riders the order in which you would like the horses to be. Tell them to keep in single file and to keep up together. Explain that when you are going to trot or canter, or if there is a hazard to avoid, you will warn the rider behind you, and each rider in turn should pass the message back down the line. If you are going to cross any roads, tell them the procedure that will be followed. This may involve your co-escort standing in the middle of the road to hold up traffic while you lead the ride across. Tell the riders that they must all cross together, the ride must never be split on either side of the road.

f. Your co-escort should understand that their job is to bring up the rear of the ride and make sure that the whole ride keeps together. If the co-escort needs to communicate with you, he or she can pass messages up the ride from rider to rider.

Content of the hack

a. The first part of the hack should always be in walk. This gives horses and riders a chance to warm-up and settle in. If it is an instructional hack, your co-escort could take the lead file for a while, and you could work your way along the line checking rider positions and giving each rider a positional correction to work on.

b. Obviously, each ride will be different, but the best place for the first trot of the hack, would be a long fairly straight track with a smooth surface. Hacking out gives riders a chance to sustain a forward-going trot for a longer period than they may be able to achieve in the school. If you are on a track enclosed by hedges or trees on either side, the horses are more likely to keep a controlled single file order. If you are instructing the riders, they could be told to check which diagonal they are on, and to change the diagonal for the next trot. Make sure you tell the riders you are about to trot, so they can prepare themselves, and then warn them when you are about to walk again.

c. Both horses and riders will be more comfortable if they use a forward position for canter work. Part of your instructional hack could include checking the position they should take up for canter. You could work your way along the line, while the riders are in walk, checking position and giving demonstrations to the riders where necessary.

d. The ideal place for a canter would also be on an enclosed track where the horses will be encouraged to keep single file. It is best if you can trot for a fairly long stretch first, and then move on into canter, rather than just bursting into canter from the walk. If the canter track is slightly uphill, this will also help to keep the horses working in a controlled fashion. Again, warn the riders that they need to prepare for canter, and tell them when you are returning to trot.

e. During any trot and canter sessions, you will need to keep looking over your shoulder to check that all is well behind you.

f. In general you should try to include a couple of canter sessions during the ride, as most riders will particularly look forward to this. Too much cantering can make the horses rather excitable, and can tire riders so they become less able to keep control. Plenty of trotting can be included if tracks are suitable. Never canter towards home or when near home, as you are likely to create a stampede. Always walk for the last ten to fifteen minutes so horses and riders return home calm and cool.

g. If the group are quite experienced and capable of jumping, then jumps which you know to be safe could be included in the hack. However, it is not a good idea for you or your co-escort to jump, as if one of you has an accident, there is no one left to look after the ride. Conduct any jumping in a controlled manner, by seeing the riders jump individually, rather than letting them follow as a ride, when things may get out of control. Never jump anything that you haven't checked carefully first. In other words, make sure you know what is on the landing side, as well as what is on the take-off.

h. More experienced riders can practise movements like leg-yielding, when out on an instructional hack. Using a straight track, they can leg-yield from one side to the other, making good use of the horse's more forward-going attitude when out of the school environment. Practical use of the turn on the forehand can also be employed, if any gates need to be negotiated.

The country code

1. Make sure you do not ride on footpaths or pavements when out on a hack. Keep to bridle paths and areas that you have permission to ride in.
2. If you meet other riders coming in the opposite direction, always walk past them and be polite. If you catch up other riders going in the same direction, ask if you can pass them and do so at a walk, or take an alternative route.
3. If you go through any gateways, always close the gate behind you, unless it has obviously been hooked open for a purpose.
4. If you have permission to ride in a field with a crop growing, ride at walk around the edge.
5. If you have permission to ride through a field with livestock in, avoid the livestock and keep to a walk.
6. If you meet any pedestrians, make sure they know you are there, by giving a friendly greeting, then take a wide berth as you pass them, and keep to a walk.
7. When car drivers take care to pass you slowly and carefully, smile and thank them for doing so.
8. Wear fluorescent and reflective clothing for roadwork so you are highly visible.
9. Do not ride on grass verges. There are likely to be hidden items of rubbish that are a potential danger to the horse. If passing cars see you riding on the verge they are unlikely to pass slowly or with a wide berth, and your horse could shy out on to the road. If you are walking on the road, then you could sidestep on to the verge in an emergency. Certainly don't canter along wide grass verges, however tempting. If

your horse shies when you are going at speed, it could easily step out on to the road before you can regain control.

10. When riding past gardens and peoples' homes, be constantly on the look out for anything that may cause your horse to take fright. For example, a person or a dog moving behind a hedge that you can see but your horse is unable to see clearly.

11. Try not to cause an obstruction. Keep to single file on narrow lanes. If you are part of a large ride, move into double file on wide roads, as car drivers will find it easier to pass a wider but short line of horses, rather than a long narrow line.

Points to note

1. If you have a group of riders that regularly attends your riding school to go out hacking, it would be a good idea to encourage the members of the group to take the Riding and Road Safety Test. In training for and passing this test, they will learn the correct procedure to follow when riding on roads, and generally improve their riding skills. This should make your job easier and the lives of the horses and other riders safer. The Riding and Road Safety Test involves the riders in turning out themselves and their horse in safe and practical equipment, riding through a simulated road test with hazards to negotiate, answering a question paper, and then going out on a real road test. The Riding and Road Safety Test is a prerequisite for the BHS Stage II examination and Pony Club C Test.

2. It is never a good idea to go hacking alone, although many people do. It would be best to go in a group of a minimum of three, so one person can stay with an injured member of the group, and one can go for help. Whatever the numbers in the group, or if you are going alone, always tell someone the approximate route you intend to take, and how long you expect to be out. If an accident should happen, and the horse returns to the yard without you, someone will know where to begin looking for you. If you don't return within the intended time, someone will be alerted to the fact that there may be something wrong and, again, can come looking for you.

3. When escorting groups of riders, always make sure the riders are of

equal ability. If for any reason the abilities are mixed (for example, a group of friends wanting to ride together), always keep the ride to the level of the least able rider. Never split the ride and send some riders for a canter while others walk; it is a recipe for disaster as horses soon become agitated if split up.

4   If you are taking a group of novices for a hack, four to six riders would be a suitable number for yourself and your co-escort to manage. If riders are more experienced, you could increase the numbers a little to perhaps eight riders plus the two escorts. However, remember this is a long string of horses to control on the roads, so make sure you do not need to do a lot of roadwork with a group this size.

5. If you have access to riding in fields, be aware that horses are more inclined to get excited in wide open spaces. Keep to the edge of the field and keep to the single file rule, otherwise horses are likely to begin trying to race past each other.

6. If riders cause harm to other people or property, they could be liable to pay damages. It is therefore a good idea for riders to be insured. Make riders aware of this fact, and advise them that if they become full members of the British Horse Society their membership will include third-party public liability insurance.

7. If the riders you take out only come to the school for hacking, try to encourage them to take lessons as well. Their riding skills are bound to be in need of improvement, and it will benefit your horses and riding school if the riders take lessons. Explain to them that it will increase their enjoyment of hacking out if aspects of their riding skills are improved.

8. If you are leading a horse and rider when mounted, always make sure the led horse is on your nearside, kept under control between yourself and the verge when on the roads. The same applies if you are on foot when leading.

9. Whether you are taking an instructional hack or not, teach the riders how to turn a horse's head away from a frightening object on the verge, and use their leg aid to push its body towards the object, so preventing it from swinging its quarters out into the road.

10. If you ride through woodland where there are likely to be low branches

to negotiate, you need to make sure the riders know how to cope with these. It may seem obvious, but novice riders may never have experienced folding down onto their horses' neck, and will need to be shown what to do in order to feel confident that they can cope. At the same time, they will need to be shown that when a horse negotiates puddles and trees it doesn't allow room for its rider's legs, unless the rider uses leg aids to guide it. The rider may not be aware that many horses would rather walk around a puddle than through it. They need to be warned of this and shown what to do.

Common rider faults and problems

1. Keep a check on your riders to make sure they do not slop along with very long reins. Riders often think they can just sit and be carried along on a ride, leaving all the work to the horse. When the reins are long, and the rider not alert, the horse will "switch off" and be likely to stumble, or may suddenly take fright and shoot off with the rider out of balance and out of control. Either situation can lead to the horse or rider falling and, as a result, injury.
2. As previously mentioned, make sure your riders are fit enough for the hack. Keep a check on their progress and take frequent breaks in walk to allow them to rest. If riders get tired they will begin to grip on to the reins and saddle for security, and may frighten the horse, causing it to go faster than they can manage.

Helpful hints on exam technique

1. Taking hacks is discussed in the theory section of the PTT exam. The examiner is looking for answers that show an awareness of safety, as hacking out is one of the most potentially dangerous activities in the riding school.
2. It is very obvious to examiners, from the answers given, which candidates have actually taken part in escorting hacks. Make sure you have gained first-hand experience in this activity before you take the exam.

14 Lectures and Stable Management Instruction

There are several different ways in which this type of instruction can be given.

a. Lectures can take the form of a theory session in the classroom, using props such as an overhead projector (OHP), blackboard and chalk, or white board and pens.
b. Practical instruction can be given in the stable yard, using stable equipment, and horses, with which a demonstration can be given, followed by practical participation.
c. Sitting and watching a video can also be a helpful way of putting over information.
d. Setting a practical task that the students can complete in a given time, followed by the instructor checking and commenting, is another way of helping students to absorb information.

The instructor's equipment

a. When using a video, make sure you have set up the equipment and checked that everything is working, that everyone will be able to see, and that there is a good picture and good sound. There is nothing more distracting and unsettling than faulty equipment. It will also create a bad impression. It is a good idea to have watched the video yourself first, to check the quality and to make sure that it gives the information you had hoped for. Videos are not always perfect, and there can be mistakes made. For example, there may be a rider riding without a hat, or leading a horse without gloves, or any number of other points that you consider not to be safe practice. You may like to make a note of these, and point them out to the students as they arise, or tell the students to look out for them and see if they can spot the mistakes.

b. For classroom lectures, try to use means of putting over or illustrating information, apart from just talking. Keep the students' attention by bringing pieces of equipment to look at and handle, or pictures to discuss, etc. Again, make sure you have something to wipe a board clean with, and something to write with. Read through and organise your notes in advance. You will lose the students' attention if you are leafing through books or folders looking for pictures, etc.

c. For practical lecture sessions, gather and check all the equipment required before you start. It will spoil your lecture if something you need is broken or missing. For example, you may pick up a grooming kit for a grooming lecture, but if you don't check it, you may find when you begin the lecture that the hoofpick is missing, or the curry comb is broken.

d. If you intend to give handouts with information for the students to take away, make sure you have enough for each student. Make extra copies to be on the safe side.

The location

a. If using a video or giving a classroom lecture, it is important to make sure you will have enough chairs for the number of students attending. The seating should be arranged so everyone is able to see. The room should be warm enough and well ventilated. Students will soon fall asleep if the room is "muggy" and airless, and will be uncomfortable if cold.

b. When giving practical lectures that involve bringing a horse out of the stable, make sure you are working in an enclosed area with the yard gates shut. If the horse gets loose it should not be able to escape. Consider the number of students attending the lecture session, and make sure there is enough room for them to gather around and see what is going on, but at the same time be a safe distance from the horse.

c. For practical lectures you will need to consider the weather conditions. Try to choose a covered area of the yard, if possible, in case of rain, etc. Don't crowd a large group of students into a stable with a horse, and thereby risk an accident.

d. If setting a practical task, make sure the students know what areas of the yard they can use or go into, and tell them if there are any areas they should not go into. For example, there may be a particular horse that is not safe to go into the box with.

e. When lecturing small groups it may be practical to use a feed room or tack room for the lecture, especially if the lecture subject involves feeding or tack.

Length of lecture

a. Lectures can be as short as five minutes in length, as you may have to give an individual instruction in how to do a particular task. For example, a student may need to be shown how to pick out a horse's foot, or brush a tail.

b. If you are giving a classroom lecture, then any length of time up to one hour, is probably most suitable. After an hour, students are likely to find it difficult to concentrate and will need a break.

c. Some practical sessions may be as long as two hours. If students are getting involved and taking part, they will probably find they can concentrate quite happily as long as they are interested and enjoying themselves.

d. The age range you are lecturing to must be considered. Young children will benefit from short sessions of maybe up to half an hour in length. Older, adult, students should be able to concentrate for longer.

Subject matter

a. All aspects of stable management can be covered in a combination of practical and theoretical sessions.

b. The theory side of equitation can also be covered in classroom lectures or in a lecture session combined with a practical demonstration.
c. It is quite helpful to return to the classroom to teach riders about the various school figures. These can be drawn or displayed on an OHP which will present a clear picture for the riders to hold in their mind's eye when they are actually riding the figures themselves.

Putting a lecture together

a. Any lecture can be structured in the same way as a riding lesson, as described in Chapter 2. The difference now is that a group of people, or an individual, will be looking at you, and waiting for your words and actions. In a riding lesson, the individual or group are actively involved with their attention focused on the horse, just listening to your commands and corrections.
b. You must be confident in your knowledge of the subject. You need to be able to speak fluently and convincingly. As with all teaching, you must speak clearly, making sure you do not go too fast for students to keep up, and not too slowly so that the students' attention wanders.
c. It is a good idea to have rehearsed your introductory sentence. In this way you can begin with confidence. You need to include your aims and objectives at this point. Students will understand and be more interested in a subject if they know what you are going to teach them about, and why they need to know about this subject.
d. The subject matter needs to be delivered in a clear and logical manner. Try not to jump about from point to point. Think through, when you make your plan, what part of the subject you should cover first, and break up the information into sections, so you can check that students have understood each section before you move on.
e. At the end of the lecture you should conclude by summarising the most important points. Ask the students if they have any questions so you can clear up misunderstandings or problems they have about the subject. If they do not have any questions for you, you could ask one or two questions of them, to check and confirm that they have taken in the main points made. It is also a good idea to outline what you intend

to cover in the next lecture, so students can prepare and look forward to what is coming next.

Points to note
1. When preparing and delivering a lecture you should carefully consider the level of knowledge that the students already have. It is possible to give too much information by going way beyond the level before the basics have been established. However, attention to detail is very important. To give an informative and interesting lecture to the level required, you must gather as much information as possible to put over to the students. It is the emphasis you place on the most important issues, and the extra details from your own experience, that make all the difference to your lecture. Also, including real-life examples that the students have seen or can see, will make a picture in their minds to remember. For example, if you are explaining how horses with certain characteristics develop stable vices, and you have a horse in the yard that weaves, you would use it as an example to illustrate what you mean.
2. There are different ways of asking questions that can be used to good effect. You can nominate a person, and then ask them the question. Or, you can ask the question and then nominate the person. The latter approach is the most effective when teaching a group, as the whole group will be thinking about the answer to the question while you are pausing before nominating someone to answer.
3. The main reason for asking questions is to see if students have listened to and understood what you have been saying. If you ask them "open" questions you will receive more informative answers than if you asked "closed" questions. An open question is one that requires a sentence to answer it. For example, "How does the diaphragm play a part in the breathing process?" A closed question is one that requires a one word, yes/no answer. For example, "Does the diaphragm play a part in the breathing process?"

Helpful hints on exam technique
1. In the PTT exam each candidate gives a short lecture of only four or

five minutes in length. The subjects covered should all be familiar to you. You are to imagine that you are lecturing to students preparing for the BHS Stage II, or Pony Club C Test. The examiner would like to see that you can show knowledge and understanding of the subject, that you can speak clearly and deliver a lecture at a good pace, that you use any props to good effect, that you present yourself well, and that the lecture is logical and easy to understand.

2. Although one would normally ask questions when giving a lecture, it is not a good idea to do so in the examination situation. Your fellow candidates will be the audience for your lecture, and will probably have their minds on the lecture topic they themselves have to give. If you ask questions you will probably get very little, if any, response, and this will not help you to feel confident. Wait until the end of the lecture, and then ask if anyone would like to ask you any questions.

3. Before you give your lecture there will be plenty of time to collect any props that you deem appropriate. The examination centre will provide any equipment you need.

4. You may take notes into the lecture with you, but be careful not to read from them continuously with your head down. Just note down the most important points you wish to cover, and use the notes as a guide to remind you of the order in which you intend to cover the subject.

5. You will be given your lecture subject at the beginning of the day, so you will have plenty of time to think about it. Some subjects would require an hour or more to cover in depth, so you will need to summarise the main points. For example: good and bad points of conformation. Other subjects are much smaller, and will require more detail. For example: bran, its problems and uses.

6. To be confident in your ability to give a five-minute lecturette, you must practise talking on a variety of subjects for five minutes, in front of an audience. You may think you know the subject, but until you have practised actually speaking aloud for five minutes at a time, you cannot be properly prepared for the task.

15 Riding School Organisation and Management of the Office

Riding establishments vary greatly in size. For example, some may have just ten to fifteen horses, no purpose-built riding arena, and just one or two staff, while others may have 100 horses, several indoor and outdoor arenas, and a large number of staff. Whatever the size of the establishment, it will require some set rules and guidelines in order to run safely and efficiently.

This chapter looks at the main areas of consideration with regard to teaching and looking after clients, and various ways in which matters can be organised.

The staff

a. As a member of staff you must be turned out neatly and safely. Suitable working clothing includes strong footwear. There are a number of boots now available with steel toecaps which are preferable and give good protection to vulnerable feet. Your footwear should also have soles which give good grip on yard surfaces. When handling and leading horses, gloves give good protection. Jewellery should not be worn, as it can easily get caught up, as can long hair, which is best tied back in some form. Other clothing should allow freedom of movement, without being too loose. Long sleeves give protection. Your turnout for teaching has already been covered in the earlier chapters of this book, but remember that you are representing your riding establishment and should therefore look smart at all times.

b. All members of staff should know the yard and office rules, routines, and procedures, and to whom they should go for help if they cannot deal with a client or answer questions they may be asked in the course of their duties. Clients will not necessarily realise that some staff members are less experienced than others. If you are asked a question that you cannot answer, don't try to bluff your way through or make something up. You will gain far more respect if you say you don't know and that you will find someone who can help. Ask the yard manager or chief instructor how the question should be answered.

c. The staff working and teaching in the yard are likely to be the first people to see any visitors that arrive. Anyone who is not known to you, should be approached. You should ask them if you can be of assistance, and make sure a visitor is not left to wander unattended around the yard. Visitors will not get a good impression if no one offers to help them and it could be dangerous for them to walk around unattended. It could, too, be dangerous for the yard, as the visitor may be a thief planning a robbery, taking note of equipment and location of the tack room, etc.

d. In this type of occupation it is a good idea if all staff have some first-aid training and qualification. It is reassuring to know that your fellow workers know what to do in the event of an accident.

The horses

a. Horses and ponies must be of a suitable temperament and schooled to a suitable level for the work they are to carry out. There is no point in having advanced horses if the main clientele are beginners.

b. Each establishment should decide how many hours of work a day each horse should do. This will depend upon how fit the horses are, which will in turn depend on how much work they do on a regular basis. It will also depend on the type of work. Horses and ponies used for beginner lessons and hacking out do not work as hard during a one-hour session as those horses used for student training and more experienced clients. Therefore, you may say that those horses working at the less intensive end of the scale can work up to four hours a day, while those working at the more advanced levels can work up to two hours a day.

c. The horses and ponies should be given variety in their work. Make sure each horse has a mixture of jumping, dressage, hacking, and lungeing if they are able. Due to age or injury, it may not be advisable to jump some horses, whilst others may have behavioural problems which prevent them from going out on hacks, but it should still be possible to give them some variety.

d. Try to distribute the horse's work fairly. There are bound to be some horses that are more popular than others, but they should not end up carrying a heavier work burden as a result. Also, split up each horse's hours as evenly as possible through the day. For example, two hours in the morning and two in the afternoon, if possible.

e. For each horse keep a horse record card, perhaps on a computer, or in files in alphabetical order of the horse's names. The record card should include general details on age, height, freeze mark, etc., along with any vaccination, shoeing and worming records. You will probably also need a forward planning diary, so you can write in when each horse is due for worming, shoeing, and vaccination.

f. Keep a constant check on each horse's tack, as it must be in a safe and serviceable condition. It may also be appropriate for some horses working at more advanced levels, to have both a dressage and jumping saddle, as well as a snaffle and double bridle.

The office

a. The size of the establishment will dictate what type of office is used. It may be a corner of the tack room, a small room amongst the stables, or a purpose-built area with a reception area, tack shop, and other facilities.

b. Try to locate your office or reception area at the front entrance of your establishment, so that visitors will go straight there rather than getting sidetracked into wandering around the stables. Clearly visible signs

Horse Record Card

Horse's name.... *Bramble* .... Arrived.. 6-2-95

Age.... 7 yrs   Colour.... Bay   Height.. 14 h.h.

Purchase price.. £ 750   Vaccination status.. Flu/Tet given 10-1-95

Last wormed.. 20/12/94   Last shod.. 20/12/94

Distinguishing features   Freeze Mark SBN9 ....

         Scar Nr. Fore bulb of heel. ....

....

Horse record card.

Shoeing Book

Horse's name	Date	Work done
Bramble	8/2	New Set
Jinx	8/2	New Fronts
Blodwyn	15/2	Removes

Shoeing book.

should direct the visitors to the reception area. Make sure that restricted areas are closed off by gates or fences.

c. The most basic requirements in the office area will be a telephone, a safe receptacle for keeping money in, and a bookings diary. In small establishments other records may be kept in the proprietor's house; otherwise the office is usually equipped with filing cabinets for horses' records, clients' records, accident book, shoeing book, veterinary records and equipment, first-aid equipment, spare protective equipment for client hire and, in larger establishments, all the necessities for running a business, from headed notepaper to computers.

d. In some instances there will be a full-time or part-time secretary. Small establishments will not have a full-time secretary, but most of the staff will be practiced at answering the telephone and dealing with enquiries. In this case, an outside bell for the telephone is an essential, so it can be heard from a distance, and an ansaphone will be helpful.

New clients

a. When a potential client telephones to make an enquiry about riding lessons for the first time, there are a number of questions that will need to be answered, and certain information you should make sure he or she receives.

b. Tell clients about the facilities you have available, the type of horses you can provide, the number of instructors you have, where you are located and the best route to take, what equipment you can offer for hire, and what time clients should arrive for their assessment lesson, making sure they know how much it will cost and if you operate any cancellation procedures.

c. Find out from clients, their age (if they are a child), their height and weight, their riding experience (if any), their name, address and telephone number, and whether they have any particular goals. For example, they may be booking a lesson to improve their riding skills so they can enjoy a riding holiday they have booked for next year. Also, tactfully ask if they have any health problems, like asthma, or anything

Client Record Card

Name   Age *14 yrs*   Date *6/2/95*

Mary Phillips   Height *5ft. 4ins*   Weight *8st. 6 lbs*

Address   Telephone

Bramble Cottage   (home) *01734 403953*

Beenham, Berks.   (business)

Riding experience *P.C. C⁺ Test, preparing for B Test.*

Regular instructor *Philly Davis*

Client record card.

else, so the instructor knows and can take this into account during the lesson.

d. Advise the clients on suitable clothing. For those that sound very keen, suggest that they don't buy any equipment yet, if this is their first riding experience, until they have given riding a try. Explain that you can hire out to them a riding hat, which they must wear. They should wear boots or shoes that have a fairly flat sole, and a block heel. Nothing with thickly-ridged soles, large buckles, wedge or high heels, and definitely not trainers. They should wear trousers that allow freedom of movement, nothing very tight or baggy. Jeans are not a good idea, as the inner seam can cause rubbing. Tracksuit trousers or thick leggings are suitable. They should also wear a top with long sleeves that is not too baggy, and gloves.

e. If they would like advice on what equipment may be necessary in the future, you should tell them that a riding hat of the most up-to-date BSI standard is the first and most important requirement, then a pair of riding boots, and then a pair of jodhpurs. A riding whip will be helpful at some point. Other items like gloves, coats, etc., they are likely to have anyway. If they become a serious rider in the future they can go on to purchase specific riding equipment if they wish. If a parent is making enquiries for their child, you could also suggest that they may like to equip them with a body protector. Advise them to buy the most important items as soon as they feel sure they would like to take up riding on a regular basis.

f. All new clients should have an assessment lesson on their first visit to the establishment. Explain to the client that this enables you to select suitable horses for them in the future, and a suitable instructor. If they are hoping to receive group instruction, the assessment will also enable you to choose a suitable group for them to join. If a new client is hoping to go out on a hack, he or she must still have an assessment lesson, as their own interpretation of their riding ability cannot be relied upon. If the client is reluctant to be assessed, choose your words carefully and you should be able to win them round. For example: "It is the riding school policy, Mr Smith, to assess all new riders, for just ten minutes or so. Then we can be sure of selecting the most suitable horses available for you, as we would like to be sure that you will gain maximum enjoyment from your hack."

g. Set up a file system, so all new clients are immediately put on a client record card. This may be a computer system, or a simple card index with clients filed by name alphabetically. There is nothing more frustrating or embarrassing than not being able to contact a client, then having them turn up for a lesson when their instructor is not available or there is a problem with the horses. Along with name and address and telephone number, you can record their riding ability, height, weight, age, and any other relevant facts. In this way, if their usual instructor is away ill, and you are going to teach them, but don't know who they are, you can find out from their record card or file.

h. Try to match up new clients with an instructor who will teach them on a regular basis in future. By developing a client/instructor relationship you will encourage the client to become a regular rider. They will look forward to seeing their instructor each week, and gain confidence in knowing that one person is taking care of their progress. When an instructor knows a client, they can choose suitable horses for them to ride and continue each lesson from where they left off the week before.

Booking systems

a. The daily routine of a riding school will probably revolve around the "Bookings" book. This book can take the form of a simple diary, or a book specifically laid out to suit the establishment.

b. The information recorded needs to include the name of the person and time of the lesson. There also needs to be a system for noting when payment is made.

c. Which horse each client is to ride, and which instructor is teaching the lesson also needs to be considered. In a small establishment there may only be one instructor, so only one lesson takes place at a time. In this case it is easy to see how many riders can be booked in and how many horses and ponies are available. There are also probably set times and days when lessons of a particular standard take place.

d. In larger establishments more involved systems need to be developed to make sure horses are not overworked and instructors are not double booked.

e. It is generally better to take payment for lessons in advance for the following week, and before each lesson begins. Once a client has had their lesson it is easy for them to forget to go and pay, or forget to book in for next week. If you take money in advance, then you can establish a system for taking part payment for any lessons cancelled without sufficient notice.

f. Make sure you have a clear system for recording when a client has paid. No one likes to be accused of not having paid when they have, so make sure there is no confusion. You need a secure, lockable, place to keep all payments as they are made.

Bookings Diary   Date 6/2

9.00 a.m. Instructor: *Philly D.* Group: *Nov. Adult* Client/Horse:	10.00 a.m. Instructor: *John K.* Group: *Beg. Child* Client/Horse:	11.00 a.m. Instructor: *Philly D.* Group: *Adv. Adult* Client/Horse:
John — Megan	Emma — Snowy	Vivien — Venture
Phillip — Jinx	Milly — Tubs	Yvonne — Jinx
Karen — Blodwyn	Fiona — Bingo	Bob — Rummy
Jill — Venture	John — Smokey	Paul — Sage
Sarah — Bas	Susan — Patches	
	Rory — Eccles	

Bookings diary.

g. You can encourage clients to have lessons on a regular basis by offering discounts for block bookings, or making offers such as one free lesson with every ten paid for in advance.

Client progress

a. As your riding establishment gains more clients, it is a good idea to begin using some type of grading system. This helps when organising riders into groups of a similar standard, and gives the clients a feeling of having achieved and improved as they work their way up the grades.

b. The BHS has a system which can be used by any riding school, called

Bookings Diary		Date
Horse	Client's name	Time
Bas	Sarah	9.00
Bingo	Fiona	10.00
Blodwyn	Karen	9.00
Eccles	Rory	10.00
Jinx	Phillip	9.00
Megan	John	9.00
Patches	Susan	10.00
Rummy	Bob	11.00

Alternative bookings diary.

the Progressive Riding Tests. The tests include stable management as well as riding, starting from the most basic upwards. Certificates are issued, to which stickers are added as the rider passes each test. The tests can be run by the school's own staff.

c. Alternatively, a riding school could devise their own series of tests. Whatever system you use, it is bound to be good for the business, as clients will be encouraged to attend regularly, or take extra instruction, in order to keep up with their tests and fellow riders. Each client's progress can be entered in their file or record card.

d. Another way of encouraging and improving riders, is to offer riding holidays or courses. One- or two-week holidays are particularly popular with children. They can travel from home each day, or stay on site if there are suitable facilities and supervision. This will improve the children's riding skills and their care and management of the horse skills – which are often neglected if children just come to ride once a week.

e. Some schools offer days or weeks when children can experience what it would be like to own a pony. They are allocated a pony and take care of it as if it were their own. This would be very good preparation if their parents were considering buying them a pony, and very good for your business if they intended to keep the pony with you.

f. Courses for adults could be for one day, a week, or one day a week spread over several weeks. Evening courses are also popular. For example, clients can attend one evening a week for one hour's riding and one hour's stable management instruction.

g. Remember that riders attending holiday weeks or courses are bound to progress more quickly than those who can only ride once a week. This may mean that group lessons need rearranging to keep riders of the same standard together.

Accident procedure

a. First, remain calm, as it is important to think clearly.

b. Make the situation safe, by telling the whole ride to halt, and send someone to catch the loose horse, while you approach the casualty. (When teaching, there are likely to be friends or relations of riders watching, who could be sent to get help. Ask one of them to get help if you think it will be necessary.)

c. Go to the casualty. Reassure him or her and tell them to keep still.

If the casualty is conscious

1. Encourage them to breathe deeply and calmly. (They may be winded and panicking about getting air.)

2. Ask them if there is any pain. Can they move their fingers and toes? Look to see if their arms and legs seem to be in a natural position.

3. Make a mental note of what they say: it will be helpful information to give the doctor or ambulance staff, should they be needed.

4. Keep talking to them. If they appear to be talking nonsense, they may have concussion and will need to be taken to a doctor.
5. If they cannot move their fingers or toes or have pain in their neck, back or limbs, do not move them. Ask for an ambulance to be called. Keep them warm with a blanket. Do not try to remove their hat or boots, etc.
6. Obvious bleeding should be stemmed by applying light pressure with a handkerchief or clean pad.
7. If the casualty feels fine and wants to get up, allow them to do so on their own. Stand nearby in case they feel faint and need support. Do not allow them to remount if you feel there is any chance they may faint. Allow them to walk for a while.

If the casualty is unconscious
1. Check there is no blockage in their mouth that may prevent them breathing and carefully loosen any tight clothing around their neck.
2. Do not move them. Send for an ambulance. Anyone who has been unconscious must be examined by a doctor in case of damage to the skull.
3. Keep talking to them; this may help to bring them round. Keep them warm.
4. Remain calm. Reassure the other pupils in your ride as soon as you can. Once the casualty has been taken to hospital, you may resume the lesson if appropriate.

Further points

a. Be prepared for accidents. Have the telephone number of your local doctor and vet clearly displayed by the telephone. Dial 999 for an ambulance. Have a first-aid kit on the yard and one that can be taken out when hacking.
b. If you have a pay phone, keep money for emergencies in an obvious place beside it. When hacking, take money for the phone.
c. If an accident occurs on the road, someone should be posted on either side to redirect traffic. If you do not have a mobile phone yourself,

there is a chance a motorist with a car phone who will be able to summon help will stop. It is obviously important to catch the loose horse as it may cause further accidents. On return to the yard, you should fill in a BHS Accident Report Form. This helps the Road Safety Development Officer of the BHS to compile statistics on road accidents involving horses.

d. If an accident involves injury to human and horse, take care of the human first but attend to the horse or send someone else to do so as soon as possible.

e. After any accident, write the details in the yard accident book.

Points to note

1. When hiring equipment for client use, make sure you take care to check the fitting of the equipment, and only offer items in good condition. Hats should be of the most up-to-date BSI or European standard. These safety standards are currently being updated. At the moment (1977), the PAS 015 is the standard offering most protection. The BHS and all the different disciplines are likely to publish the recommended or required standards in the near future. Hats should fit snugly on the head, without being uncomfortably tight, and not be loose.

2. If clients arrive unsuitably clothed for a lesson, you must have an agreed policy on what to do. Tactfully explain that their clothing is not safe for riding, or that the jewellery they are wearing is likely to be dangerous and cause an injury. Where possible, offer alternative clothing, such as boots, and ask them to remove jewellery. If the client will not change their footwear or remove, for example, a bracelet, then you will have to tell them that they will not be able to ride. Do not accept responsibility for their jewellery; ask them to take care of it themselves.

3. Each instructor should accept a certain amount of responsibility for their clients. The instructor is the link between the client and any information recorded in the office, and will be trusted by the client to give good instruction and advice. You take on responsibility when you are an instructor, which should never be underestimated, or taken lightly. There should be a chief instructor who takes on overall responsibility

for the staff. They should be there to give guidance and answer questions, making sure that everyone is working along the same lines.

Helpful hints on exam technique

1. Part of the theory section of the PTT exam will be devoted to questions on business knowledge of the type covered in this chapter. The examiner would like to hear answers which show that the candidate has some real experience in this area. If you answer using examples of the systems used in the riding school where you work, this experience will show. However, remember that there are many different types of school, and different systems will be used in different places. All are acceptable if they work.

2. When answering questions on accident procedure, which will also be covered in the theory section, remember that each situation requires slightly different action. The examiner is trying to find out if you have general knowledge on what action to take, and that you will be able to adapt the procedure to different situations.

Index

Page numbers in italics refer to illustrations